Amy Zerner & Monte Farber

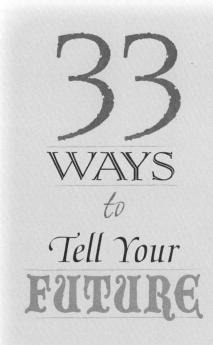

33 WAYS to Tell Your FUTURE

Astrology
Palmistry
Tea Leaf Reading
Crystal Ball
Dowsing
Numerology
and much more!

Tune In, Get Answers, and Predict!

STERLING ETHOS
An imprint of Sterling Publishing Co., Inc.

New York / London
www.sterlingpublishing.com

33 Ways to Tell Your Future

Text copyright © Amy Zerner & Monte Farber 2010
This edition copyright © Zerner/Farber Editions 2010

Published by:
Sterling Publishing Co., Inc.
387 Park Avenue South
New York, NY 10016-8810

For information, address
The Enchanted World of Amy Zerner & Monte Farber
Post Office Box 2299, East Hampton, NY 11937 USA
E-mail: info@TheEnchantedWorld.com
Website: www.TheEnchantedWorld.com

Library of Congress Cataloging-in-Publication Data available on request.
ISBN: 978-1-4027-2950-8
First U.S. edition published 2010
9 8 7 6 5 4 3 2 1

Graphic design by Rose Sheifer-Wright

Many thanks to MaryJane Seely for her valuable assistance.

For information about custom editions, special sales, premium and
corporate purchases, please contact Sterling Special Sales
Department at 800-805-5489 or specialsales@sterlingpub.com

Printed in China through Colorcraft Ltd., Hong Kong

For entertainment purposes only.

Contents

Introduction

Fortune-telling is fun; I should know—I've made my living doing it and writing about it for decades. My name is Monte Farber, and I first learned the art of predicting the future when I met my future wife, Amy Zerner, the artist, fashion designer, and co-author of this book. At the time, Amy was studying astrology and reading Tarot cards, and I was studying Amy, so I learned astrology and the Tarot!

Back then I thought that it was impossible to tell the future, but, as the great British scientist Sir Thomas Huxley said, "I'm too much of a skeptic not to believe that anything is possible," and so I gave astrology and the Tarot a fair hearing and soon found out that there was something to them—a lot, actually. I learned that I could predict future events in my life!

As the old adage says, "Forewarned is forearmed," and so my knowledge of the probable future conditions I was going to experience allowed me to better prepare for them. I know that this sounds a bit out there, but try it for yourself and you'll see what I mean; you'll also have a lot of fun, and everyone will want to be read by you and invited to your parties. I have a good sense of humor, and I used to sing and play the guitar, and while those are certainly great ways to become popular with your social set, they are no match for having the ability to tell people about their future—not even close!

We've written *33 Ways to Tell Your Future* as a thorough compendium of easy-to-use and enjoyable methods for fortune-telling, because each of us naturally gravitates to one or more of these fascinating techniques, but not necessarily all of them. If you have *33 Ways to Tell Your Future* on your coffee table, you've got fortune-telling covered.

Even if a person doesn't believe it's possible to tell the future, there's hardly anyone who isn't interested in giving it a try, because it's so much fun. Take a room full of strangers and let them try a few of the techniques described in this book, and you'll find that they start to share their stories with one another as if they've been friends for years.

Another thing I've learned beyond doubt over the years is that there's nothing more powerful than our human free will. There's no reading so dire that it cannot be modified for the better. If you or someone else gets an answer that you are not happy with, then ask additional questions whose goal is to help you change the future. That's another thing I'm certain of; the future can be changed when we use our free will, guided by what we think the future may be. I know because I've done it and I've advised many people on how to do it. Conversely, there's no reading that is so great that it cannot be diminished or negated entirely by a person's actions or inaction.

When I first realized that there was something to fortune-telling, I learned the truth of another old adage: "Knowledge is power." Having greater power over my life and making better, more informed decisions was something I liked and wanted more of. I became hungry to know more. I learned all I could about foretelling the future, got really good at it, and found to my surprise that as my reputation spread, I was invited to every party imaginable out here in the "fabulous Hamptons," and why not? After all, I can predict the future much more accurately than chance, and now that you have our book in your hands, you, too, have *33 Ways to Tell Your Future*—yours and that of your friends, family, and fellow party people, whether at your party or theirs.

The most successful among us are usually the ones who are best at predicting what the future will be. Down through history right up until today, the world's rich, famous, and powerful have discretely consulted readers who are expert at one or more of our book's thirty-three methods to help them stay that way or even increase their wealth, fame, and power. The techniques you are about to learn and enjoy in *33 Ways to Tell Your Future* are not called "fortune-telling" for nothing. Using them can help you to make your fortune.

The legendary financier J.P. Morgan, a man whose holdings were worth billions of dollars at a time in America's history when you could eat like a king for a couple of dollars, once famously replied to someone questioning his inclusion of the advice of astrologers in his decision-making mix, "Millionaires don't use astrology; billionaires do."

I would be remiss, however, if I did not point out that in my many years of doing readings for

people, their first and most important questions are invariably about love and romance. This is why we've made sure that all of our techniques are geared to both relationships and improving one's financial health.

I am always surprised when someone asks me, "Do you really think it's possible for a human being to predict the future?" Of course it is. Each day since human beings first walked the Earth, each person has made his or her short- and long-range plans based on what he or she believes the future will be, the very definition of predicting. Daydreaming about, predicting, and planning for the future is how we spend a significant portion of every day, and, thankfully, it has always been so. To not do so would practically guarantee a shortened and difficult life filled with panicked efforts to cope with unforeseen circumstances.

The use of any and all of the thirty-three ways to tell your future described here may actually produce an added bonus. Using the fortune-telling methods in this book may, over time, improve your intuition, a very valuable ability to add to your own decision-making mix. This is obviously true of those who make successful decisions regarding business, investments, and other forms of financial risk taking, but it is also true at a much more everyday level.

I once asked Amy what she thought was the common denominator in all human-caused suffering, and she replied without hesitation, "Poor decision making." I was astounded by her insight, as I often am. How many times have we said to ourselves, "I should have gone with my first impression," or "I should have listened to that little voice that was trying to tell me what to do"? Not only is this book, *33 Ways to Tell Your Future*, great fun to use, especially in social situations, but using it regularly will help you to improve your ability to hear that little voice; it certainly helped me do exactly that.

I have devoted my life to the study of methods for predicting the future. I am, with Amy, the author of a best-selling series of richly illustrated books and metaphysical teaching systems that have sold more than two million copies in fourteen languages. All of them are dedicated in one way or another to helping you to predict your future. But *33 Ways to Tell Your Future* is the first and only all-in-one book we've written that puts the best and most fun methods we know and use ourselves into one easy-to-use and surprisingly powerful guidebook.

Today, I not only write about methods for predicting the future; I am one! I am a professional psychic, possessed of an ability whose development I partially credit to the thousands of readings I've done for people as an astrologer and a Tarot reader, using Amy's gorgeous *Enchanted Tarot*, *Zerner/Farber Tarot*, and *True Love Tarot* decks, of course.

But I was not born psychic. It was through my studies, my counseling practice, the writing of our books, and, most important, my use of our various systems for predicting the future and improving one's intuition that I have reached my present level of psychic ability.

How I wish I had had this book when I was first starting my journey of self-improvement; I would have developed so much sooner the innate psychic ability that we all have within us! Most of the books available when we started out were quite old and were written in an old-fashioned style, which I enjoyed and have emulated on occasion throughout *33 Ways to Tell Your Future* to remind you that there is a rich history to the techniques revealed to you in its pages.

Writing *33 Ways to Tell Your Future* has helped me to fulfill what I consider to be the meaning of my life, that is, to help other people give meaning to their lives as Amy and I have. So even though you've been attracted to this book by its cover and the promise of lots of fun, which it can fulfill and then some, you are now holding in your hand a method for improving your decision-making ability and, therefore, every aspect of your life. Who knows? You might find that your own psychic gift is there inside you, waiting for a bit of practice to help you let it out without feeling that it's weird or spooky.

When you have fun using the wonderful and enlightening techniques in this book, remember that doing so connects you to the unbroken chain of people who have also used them down through the ages. The reason that we have astrology is because our distant ancestors watched the planetary movements to observe and predict the timing of events and cycles, like the seasons, the fortunes of nations, and their leaders.

Like astrologers, people of all races and nationalities have devised methods of "divining" the future. *Divining*, in fact, is a word whose origin reminds us that all of these methods were designed to put us in touch with the Divine. Each of the Earth's peoples has created their own way for using the available clues in the world around them to map out a greater truth. Down through time, when people sought to discover meaning through the letters in a name or in the

Introduction

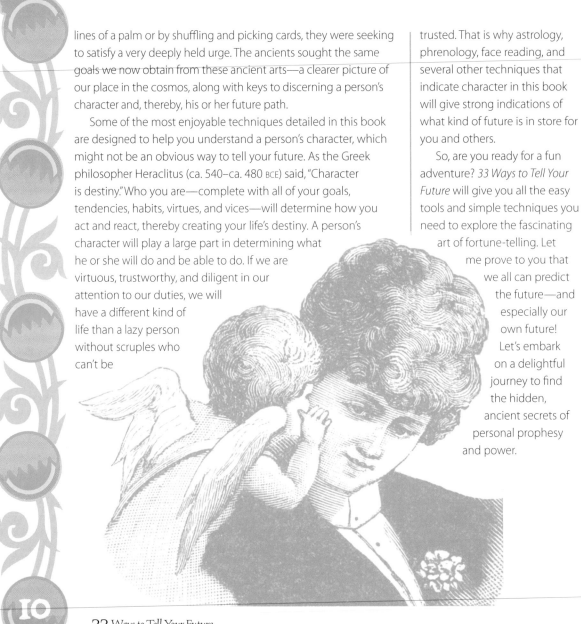

lines of a palm or by shuffling and picking cards, they were seeking to satisfy a very deeply held urge. The ancients sought the same goals we now obtain from these ancient arts—a clearer picture of our place in the cosmos, along with keys to discerning a person's character and, thereby, his or her future path.

Some of the most enjoyable techniques detailed in this book are designed to help you understand a person's character, which might not be an obvious way to tell your future. As the Greek philosopher Heraclitus (ca. 540–ca. 480 BCE) said, "Character is destiny." Who you are—complete with all of your goals, tendencies, habits, virtues, and vices—will determine how you act and react, thereby creating your life's destiny. A person's character will play a large part in determining what he or she will do and be able to do. If we are virtuous, trustworthy, and diligent in our attention to our duties, we will have a different kind of life than a lazy person without scruples who can't be

trusted. That is why astrology, phrenology, face reading, and several other techniques that indicate character in this book will give strong indications of what kind of future is in store for you and others.

So, are you ready for a fun adventure? *33 Ways to Tell Your Future* will give you all the easy tools and simple techniques you need to explore the fascinating art of fortune-telling. Let me prove to you that we all can predict the future—and especially our own future! Let's embark on a delightful journey to find the hidden, ancient secrets of personal prophesy and power.

Teacup Fortune-Telling

Can you see the man in the Moon? Can you see the Big Dipper when it is pointed out in the starry heavens? If you can, you can also read tea leaves. The forms taken by leaves in the bottom of a teacup after you've drunk the tea are not always so clear as an artist's sketch or so realistic as a photograph, but with a little help from your imagination, you can see stars, crowns, crosses, snakes, daggers, circles, mountains, and other marvelous things in tea leaves. All such forms have meanings, which provide revealing insights about the past, present, and future.

Practically anyone can read tea leaves. It is easy to imagine that a ring shape may mean marriage; that a snake symbolizes transformation; that a path signifies a journey. For instance, if you find a snake lying across a path pictured in tea leaves, your deduction could be "I see a journey coming up; you will be required to deal with an obstacle to your goals and doing so will transform you for the better." If you see a ring and near it a long path, the interpretation might be "I see a long and happy marriage. Or it could be a long engagement leading up to a happy marriage."

Use Your Imagination

Give your imagination full rein when interpreting tea leaves. We do not mean that you should say just anything that pops into your mind; that can be done only by those with years of experience. You should inspect the leaves carefully; observe what symbols are to be found in them; then search in your own thoughts for any ideas, intuitions, or feelings you may have about those symbols. Only then, taking care to include what you know about the circumstances of person you are reading for and the person's ability to handle what you may be about to say, should you express those ideas.

Some people claim that they see far beyond the simple little tea leaves left in the bottom of a cup. They see the leaves and immediately identify the symbols, locating the rings, crosses, paths, crowns, snakes, and so on. They put them all together easily, and their intuition or imagination is able to elaborate on the result in great detail. You may be one of these people! In any case, say what you see, and remember—it's what the symbol means to you that is your answer. The extensive list below is what the symbols have come to mean for us, but you may interpret some or all of them differently, depending on your life's experience.

If possible, use a white cup. Make the tea using loose black or green tea—not in tea bags, please. Add hot water. Then, when the tea has cooled enough to drink, have the subject drink the cup practically dry. Tell him or her to turn the cup around three times, clockwise, while making a wish and using a swinging motion to spread the leaves as much as possible. Then the subject should turn the cup upside down on a saucer. You, the reader, then turn the cup right side up and examine it carefully. The tea leaves will cling to the sides and bottom of the cup in a unique formation.

Proceed slowly. Look at all the leaves from all directions. At first you may find it difficult to discover what shapes the leaves resemble. Practice will make it easy for you to weave a fortune out of the leaf formations. Don't expect the leaves to resemble various objects with photographic accuracy. Above all, concentrate sympathetically on the fortune seeker.

His or her wish will be granted if the leaves form a straight line in any direction. If they make a half circle, the answer is "no." If there are no such formations, uncertainty as to the fulfillment of the wish is indicated.

The top of the cup represents the present. A path lying near the top of the cup means a trip in the immediate future or a trip just completed.

The handle of the cup is the home. A basket (symbol of a gift) near the handle means a gift for the home.

Leaves near the top of the cup are "happier" leaves than those at bottom. For example, a cat near the top of the cup means domestic content; a cat at the bottom of the cup means a sort of betrayal is present.

Leaves to the left of the handle indicate events passed; leaves to the right, events in the future or present.

Following is a list of interpretations for many common formations of the leaves:

Simple Geometric Symbols

CIRCLE: After years of effort, are you still where you started? Analyze yourself, determine your failings, and try to avoid them in the future.

CRESCENT: Romance. No ordinary love affair this, but a relationship with the added charm of strangeness—perhaps a meeting in a strange land.

CROSS: Perhaps you are coming to a crossroads or turning point in your life, where a wise decision will mean happiness such as you have never yet experienced.

CROSS WITHIN A CIRCLE: The approaching turning point in your life is surrounded by indecision. A lucky unexpected event may guide you better than a deliberate choice on your own part.

DASHES: You are approaching a period of great excitement. Enjoy the thrills, but the leaves caution you to keep your head!

DOTS: The confetti symbol; a promise of enjoyable times to come.

DOTS AND DASHES: A message will bring you news that will have a marked effect on your life.

ELONGATED S: The sign of beauty. If you are a man, you are about to meet someone unbelievably lovely; if you are a woman, you, yourself, by daily care, and by preserving a cheerful disposition, will attain an attractiveness you never thought possible.

OBLONG: The suggestion of a box. Are you hiding something from someone? Is something being hidden from you?

OVAL: Are you proud and swaggering? The leaves prophesy an encounter that may take the wind out of your sails.

PARALLEL LINES: A road. You are going on a journey—actual or spiritual—and your goal is far from home.

SERPENTINE LINE: You are about to experience an infatuation for someone of the opposite sex.

SQUARE: Something of great importance will happen to you in the near future while you are standing on a street corner. The event may be a meeting with one who will come to mean a lot to you, or it may concern itself with something you will see there.

STAR: The sign of spirituality. Are you at last finding consolation in your faith?

STRAIGHT LINES: How fortunate you are—how straight the course to your heart's desire!

TRIANGLE: Are you part of one of those turbulent love relationships known as a triangle? If so, then remember not to show any sign of jealousy. By a clever strategy you may yet win out.

Punctuation Marks and Monetary Symbols

CENTS SIGN: You are very economical with small things, but you are likely to spend freely on the things that really count.

DOLLAR SIGN: You can expect to be accumulating money or material things soon, as long as you know true happiness is not to be found there.

EXCLAMATION POINT: Excitement. Your heart may well skip a beat—the leaves predict for you the most thrilling time of your life.

QUESTION MARK: Uncertainty. The outcome of the issue you have been holding most dear is very doubtful. You are at the mercy of another's will.

Inanimate Objects

AIRPLANE: Your hopes may well go soaring, for an excellent opportunity may soon present itself to you.

ANCHOR: Doubts, distractions, and wanderings are nearly over. A haven of peace and contentment lies in sight. This is also the sign of trade and travel.

APPLE: Discord. If you don't want this image to take effect, you'd better deal with the irritability of your partner or teacher with a special graciousness.

ARROW: The trouble with you is that you have too many interests. Take the arrow symbol as a hint to choose a definite direction—you will then more readily arrive at your goal.

BASKET: You have the gift within you of being content and will always have enough to live on.

BELL: A summoning. Perhaps it is to court that you will be summoned, perhaps to the house of a friend.

BOAT: At last a complete change is to come into your life. The joys of an ocean voyage or travel in a foreign country may be yours. An important meeting may occur while you are traveling.

BOOK: You will soon meet someone whom you can attract only by being well-read and knowledgeable about current events.

BOOT: You must travel a long way to find what you want.

CAGE: This symbol bids you beware of imprisonment, perhaps in a loveless relationship.

CANDLE: Revelation. The leaves predict that you will discover something that will astonish you.

CHAIR: This sign foretells a meeting between friends. It may influence your love life or your career. Make the most of it.

CLOCK: On your punctuality at a certain function in the near future, much may depend.

BOUQUET	STAR	MOON	SNAKE	HORSESHOE
HAPPINESS	LOVE	ROMANCE	ENEMY	GOOD-LUCK

CLOUDS: Small, light clouds mean the granting of your dearest wish. If they are heavy and lowering, gloomy events may soon be upon you, but your courage will carry you through.

COMET: An event of unbelievable splendor will soon light up your life.

COMPASS: You should soon choose a new direction, for the one you now pursue will lead nowhere.

COMPUTER: You will find your true mate while doing ordinary chores, possibly online.

CROSS: If you are standing alone, your troubles will soon clear. In the thick of too many other people and opinions, more trouble could come.

CUP: The temptation of alcohol, drugs, or some other form of escapism may prove too great for you or for someone dear to you.

DAGGER: Your strong disagreement with one whom you really admire may lead to a quarrel you will both regret.

EASEL: You will fall or are in love with a creative person.

EGG: You are about to make a promise that will change the course of your life.

ENGINE: Let nothing slow down your energy or interfere with your capacity for work. The leaves symbolize that these are your most important assets.

EYE: Someone is watching you. Be careful lest you give away your secrets!

FAN: You are soon to be showered with attention that may lead to publicity.

GRAPES: Many admirers will cluster around you, but none will be true, for the time being.

GUITAR: A musician will become infatuated with you, or music will lead you to love.

GUN: The fight of your life lies ahead of you. Be on guard.

HARP: Harmony of tastes will make your relationship a happy one.

HEART: Denotes love, which is reciprocated, and joy over a gift.

HORN: Something of great importance will happen to you on a special holiday.

HOURGLASS: Your plans will ripen best if you give them plenty of time.

HOUSE: The joys of domesticity are promised to you. A happy home, an adoring mate, and a loving family—these will make you fortunate above most human beings.

JUG: You may have an unexpected windfall and have more money than you planned.

KETTLE: You will enjoy a comfortable old age.

KEY: At last you will be free! Perhaps you are acquiring a long-wanted divorce, perhaps leaving your hometown for the big city, perhaps merely conquering a fear that has hampered your movements.

KITE: Prepare for a glad lift of the heart; it will be caused either by an improvement in your own fortunes or by the happiness of one you love.

KNIFE: The sign of division. A tie that has bound you close to another is soon to be cut.

LADDER: You will make striking progress in your chosen field. It's time to ask for a raise.

LAMP: While reading or writing, you will be interrupted by a visitor or caller, whom you will resent at first, but who will mean more and more to you as time goes on.

LEAF: This sign predicts a scattering. Look to your investments, lest your money gets scattered away. Alternatively, it may mean that your team is about to break up for at least a little while.

LETTER: The emblem of a letter in the clear part of the cup brings pleasant news; if it is surrounded by dots, money is coming to you, but if the surrounding leaves are large, be ready for a disappointment.

LOCK: You are about to have an experience that you will keep secret.

MASK: Never forget that things are seldom what they seem. In the situation you are soon to face, you must play the game while at the same time penetrating all disguises to get at the truth.

MOON: Social or political prominence will come to you if the Moon stands alone. Alternatively, you may be about to fall in love. If clouds surround the Moon, there might be regret for a short period.

MOUNTAIN: Hard climbing ahead. You may get what you want, but it will not satisfy you.

MUSHROOM: Temptation will try to divert you from doing what you know you should do. Resist it with all your might.

NAILS: Building. Is it your own home you are building or renovating? This symbol also suggests that you may work at home.

NECKLACE: You will soon receive a valued gift, a symbol of admiration.

PAIL: A vacation is indicated. It could be made all the more interesting by a romantic attachment for a fellow tourist, or falling in love with a place that you visit or someone who lives there.

PILLOW: Perhaps your frequent quarrels with the person you love are due to irritability caused by overwork. Wouldn't it be a good idea to cut down on business activity and get a good rest?

PURSE: This sign promises prosperity. Perhaps it will be in the form of a legacy, but it is more likely to be the hard-earned result of your labors.

RACQUET: You are about to take part in a contest of skill or wit. The leaves admonish you to take the time to prepare yourself to win.

RING: Always means marriage or an engagement. If clear, it brings much happiness. Surrounded, it warns you to be careful about whom you can trust. Seen in the bottom of the cup, it means a separation that brings sadness for a time.

RIVER: You are fortunate in finding this sign, for it implies that your most treasured possession will be with you always.

SAW: You will, before long, find yourself deeply attached, not necessarily romantically, to one of your co-workers.

SCALES: A lawsuit may loom ahead. Seek justice. This sign also indicates that you need to be more balanced in work and play.

SCEPTER: You are due for a clash with authority. If you have nothing to fear from a representative of the law, then the most quarrelsome member of your family or friends may be the person that causes the clash.

SCISSORS: In a difficult situation you are soon to face, a designer, artist, or tailor will lend a helping hand.

SCYTHE: The harvest of your hopes will soon be ripe.

Teacup Fortune-Telling

17

SPOON: The birth of an heir—your own or that of a friend—is to be expected.

SUN: Growth. This may mean your money will increase or, at the very least, good times are coming soon.

TABLE: This sign may promise you an invitation to a party, or it may signify even more—an abundance of the things you value.

TEAPOT: You are entering upon a period of great social activity. You may be asked to be on a committee.

TELEPHONE: You will be called upon frequently. Make that call you've been putting off.

TELESCOPE: An event now taking place thousands of miles away will have an important effect on your future life.

TREE: The happiest events in your life will occur in the spring and summer of the year.

WHEEL: Karma! Fate is about to take a hand in your plans, unexpectedly helping or hindering you.

WINDOW: Escape! Real adventure is just around the corner. The leaves caution you to take care.

WINGS: Through the saintly goodness of another person, you will be saved from some difficulty.

Flower Symbols

ACORNS: Expansion and growth will come from seeds you are planting now.

BOUQUET: Do not be afraid to tell the person who has impressed you. The leaves predict that this will be your way of winning love.

CLOVER: You will forsake your present attachment for the charm of someone new.

DAFFODIL: You will do well to choose the spring for the starting point of any important enterprise.

DAISY: Lying in an open field next summer, you will have a dream that will reveal much that you have failed to understand.

IRIS: A garden will be the scene of an important romance.

IVY: In an old house you will find certain important papers that will affect your future.

LILY: As you would suppose, the lily is a sign of virtue and innocence. Seen clearly and alone, it indicates a mate with a spotless reputation, long life, and happiness, but seen in the bottom, thickly surrounded, it could indicate discouragement.

ROSE: A royal welcome awaits you where you want it most.

VIOLETS: A walk through a park, grove, or forest will lead you to your desire.

Insect Symbols

BEE: Only through being industrious can you acquire the honey you desire.

BUTTERFLY: One who is young and lovely will lead you to a happier life.

FLY: Summer will bring you your desire.

SPIDER: A trap is being prepared for you. But the leaves indicate that if you are very cautious, you will avoid falling into it.

SPIDERWEB: You will achieve your goal through the use of networking, possibly through the World Wide Web, the Internet.

Bird Symbols

CANARY: You will be separated from those you love, but if you endure the separation cheerfully, relief will come sooner than you think.

CHICKEN: Is it your own self-righteousness that is hindering your plans, or that of another?

CRANE: At a summer watering place, you will meet the love of your life.

DUCK: Your middle years will be much more contented than those of your youth.

EAGLE: You may leave those who are now your companions, for you will not be content until you have gone far beyond them.

HUMMINGBIRD: The voice that is to guide you may be only a murmur, a suggestion, but the leaves bid you to heed it well. Your intuition is trying to tell you something.

OSTRICH: Beware of the hypocrisy of one you trust.

OWL: You are at your best at night. The high spots of your next few months will occur after sundown.

PARROT: Beware that your innocent behavior might be misunderstood or become the subject of scandal.

PEACOCK: You will fall in love with one who is too vain to love anyone but him or herself.

RAVEN: Does your pessimism stand in the way of your success? Cultivate a more cheerful outlook and you will find many doors open to you.

SWALLOW: A happy home life is more to your taste than great adventure.

SWAN: A dancer or very graceful person is about to come into your life.

VULTURE: Beware of a thief or someone waiting for you to fail.

Animal Symbols

The forms of animals are often very distinctly formed by the tea leaves.

BEAR: The value of your possessions is diminishing rapidly, so be frugal.

BULL: Investments will turn out well for you.

CAMEL: You will love best the person who breaks through your exterior persona to the sweeter and more lovable traits beneath.

CAT: Someone sly stalks behind you. You must watch carefully your every move.

COW: You will soon have to make a choice between loyalty to one to whom you owe much and love for another. The leaves reveal that loyalty will probably win.

DOG: You make friends readily and keep them long. The symbol shows that this enviable talent will save you in a time of trouble.

DONKEY: Is stubbornness your greatest weakness? Does it now stand in the way of reconciliation with one you love? Forget your pride—then you will be rewarded with happiness.

FISH: Your patience will be rewarded with a good catch.

GOAT: A time of revelry and delightful abandon is at hand.

HARE: Quickness of action is a necessity. Only a speedy decision can bring you what you want.

HORSE: Are you a bearer of burdens for others? It is admirable to be kind and generous, but do not let others take advantage of you.

LAMB: Your quarrels are over—at last you are to enjoy the blessings of peace.

LION: The lust for power is your greatest ambition. Be careful lest you alienate those you care about.

LOBSTER: An untraditional beauty in the one you love will attract you as much as his or her excellent character.

MONKEY: You are destined to become a performer or an actor, or to go into politics.

MOUSE: You will be showered with the attentions of one you find boring. Be sure to discourage this person in order to leave the field clear for the true love of your life.

PIG: Success lies ahead, but you may have to endure a period of scrambling for money that is first required.

SNAIL: Slowness. Be patient. Your success will be all the more striking for taking so long to achieve.

SNAKE: Keep your eyes on each step you take. Greed and envy lurk concealed and ready to spring.

SQUIRREL: By your actions and lessons learned during your youth, your old age will be well provided for.

TOAD: A person with an unpleasant character waits for the chance to upset you.

WOLF: Someone will try to prey upon your natural generosity by demanding of you more than you should give.

The Art of Palmistry

The art of palmistry is devoted to the study of the human hand and the significance of its variation in size, shape, texture, and surface indications. The study of the hand originated in India, where it was understood and practiced, and its prophetic meanings were respected and obeyed.

It was during the ancient Greek civilization, however, that palmistry flourished, receiving the serious attention and sanction of the great philosophers of the day, among them such intellectual giants as Aristotle and Pliny. Since then, the practice of palmistry has been carried on from century to century, surviving bigotry, charlatanism, and opposition, until today it promises to reach a new golden age of interest and importance. All it will take is for more and more people to give it a try.

Palmistry, the general term covering the study of the hand, is divided into two areas:

1. *Cheirognomy*, which deals with the different shapes and types of the hand and fingers, and the hereditary effect of character and disposition
2. *Cheiromancy*, which relates to the mounts, lines, and markings of the palm, and their relation to events of the past, present, or future

Both terms are derived from the Greek word *cheir*, which means "hand."

What May Be Learned from Hands

When beginning to read someone's hand, you can readily gain a general indication of the habits and temperament of the individual in question by a careful examination of the texture or quality of the skin. As it is with all impressions gained from this and the other thirty-two fortune-telling methods in this book, the readings indicated must never be taken by themselves, but only in conjunction with other confirming signs, and then considered in light of the fact that our free will can change the future. Amazingly, those changes will often appear in one's hand.

TEXTURE OF SKIN: The skin may, of course, be smooth or rough. To judge this you should turn the hand in question so that the palm is facing down. Now get the feel of the skin by actual touch; a smooth, fine-textured skin denotes a refined nature, and vice versa. Should there be other tendencies pointing to coarseness of nature, a refined texture of the hand would have a refining effect upon the whole hand, and vice versa.

ELASTICITY OF THE HAND: This is best tested by shaking hands with the person you're reading. All hands naturally present some feeling of elasticity; this is a matter of comparison, but it is very easy to tell the quick, virile grip of an elastic hand as opposed to the "dead fish" feeling that a flabby hand gives us when we grasp it.

A FLEXIBLE HAND: A non rigid hand denotes an active and energetic person, one who will be readily adaptable to new conditions. He or she will always rise to the occasion and can withstand the challenges of hard times. This type is always trustworthy and a good friend.

A FLABBY HAND: A hand that does not respond to your grip or responds sluggishly is traditionally thought to be the hand of a undependable and inconsistent person, a person of weak and unconstructive character. Be sure to search thoroughly for other confirming signs of this weakness before rendering final judgment.

The Shape of the Hand

A fairly accurate guide to character is contained in the shape of the hand. Hands may be roughly divided into two classes—broad and long. A person having a long hand you may judge to have a great capacity for mental effort and matters of detail.

The broad-handed person you may expect to be a strong person physically; his or her approach to things will be physical rather than mental. He or she will get the job done once what is needed is clearly understood.

The Shape of the Fingers

SQUARE: When an individual is found with square fingertips, he or she should make a good and devoted marriage partner; he or she will be practical—a person of method and reason. This individual is punctual but should work on developing his or her imagination.

POINTED FINGERTIPS: These will be found on the hand of the musician, the painter, and anyone who is of artistic temperament. Persons with this fingertip shape should balance their imagination with reason and should cultivate the power of doing things in the real world in a practical way, instead of just dreaming about them.

TAPERING FINGERS: Fingers that get narrower toward the ends indicate people of extremes. "Ice and fire" are these people—impulsive and generous to a fault. They should guard against moody sensitivities and should cultivate a rational philosophical outlook upon life. They are capable of greatness but frequently are their own worst enemies.

SPATULATE FINGERS: These fingers have a narrow, tapering base and a broad, rounded tip. People with this fingertip type are the sportspersons of the world, the athletic types. They are not worried much by the opinions of others. They love a busy, healthy life, a sound mind in a sound body.

The Mounts

Take your subject's hand or your own and examine it closely. It's a good idea to use a strong magnifying glass for this examination and others that follow. It will be seen that there are certain portions of the hands that are raised above the surface. These are known as the *mounts*. As will be noticed in the accompanying picture, we call these mounts by astrological names, a method adopted from the very earliest times.

They are eight in number, named Jupiter, Mercury, Venus, Saturn, Apollo, Luna, and Mars (of which there are two).

At the base of the first finger you will see Mount Jupiter; then, taking the base of each finger in turn, will be found Mount Saturn, Mount Apollo, and Mount Mercury. Mount Luna will be found at the base of the hand, below the little finger, near the wrist, Mount Mars just above it. Mount Venus stands below Mount Jupiter and at the root of the thumb, with the second Mount Mars above it.

All individuals do not have these mounts developed to the same extent. It is in these variations where strong indications of character are to be found. Usually one of these mounts in your or your subject's hands will be found to stand out clearly from the others. This will give you a good idea of the general type of person whose hand you are reading. The excess or overdevelopment of one particular quality (however excellent this quality may be) is unbalanced. Thus, a superartistic temperament sometimes becomes neurotic, while the over-prudent person becomes the grasping miser.

Following are the general indications to be found in a reading of the mounts:

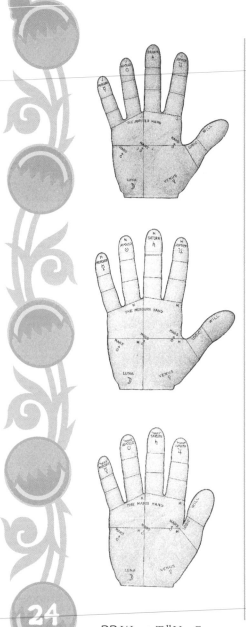

THE SATURNIAN: If the Mount of Saturn is overdeveloped, the person may be cold, skeptical, or pessimistic. He or she may lack compassion or empathy. If there is moderate development in the Mount of Saturn, this person is likely to be well-balanced; prudent, not miserly; optimistic yet realistic. Those with emphasized Mounts of Saturn often had difficult childhoods.

THE JUPITERIAN: People with an excessively strong Mount of Jupiter are often the strong people of the world. They can be overly ambitious, overbearing, and bullying. With a moderate development of this mount, exceedingly good qualities are indicated: power of leadership, rightful ambition, initiative, and great abilities for hard work.

THE APOLLONIAN: People with a strong Mount of Apollo are usually the optimists. They often have cheery natures and a love of the artistic, the tasteful, and the beautiful. The sculptors, painters, and musicians who make life so pleasant are very frequently Apollonians. The best advice to give an Apollonian is "moderation in all things." He or she must be very careful in the choice of a partner.

THE MERCURIAN: A person with the Mount of Mercury in excess can be duplicitous. In moderation, this mount usually indicates a good businessperson, shrewd and cautious, with the capacity for doing the lion's share of the work. Kindness and generosity will make a Mercurian a most charming person; their lack can leave a clever, scheming scoundrel.

THE MARTIAN: When we find an overdeveloped Mount of Mars, we usually find aggression and even bullying. With this mount in moderation, we often have a fighter in the best sense of the word, a person who can withstand the blows of fate and fight his or her way through life, resisting evil. This is almost never a mean person, and you will find him or her a sincere and trustworthy friend.

THE VENUSIAN: With the Mount of Venus in excess, we find a moody and careless person, one who often is an uncommitted partner. When this mount is developed to a moderate degree, we usually find generosity and compassion. These are the people who love love, beauty, and being with a partner; they are therefore likely to fall in love too easily. They must think before they act and be careful with their extravagances.

THE LUNARIAN: Lastly let us take the Mount of the Moon. When this mount is in excess, we can again find the neurotic or unduly nervous person. This mount in moderation indicates a Lunarian who is often a person of imagination and sympathy, one who loves to look on all that is sweet in life. He or she should be successful as a musician or writer and should have a ready capacity for learning foreign languages.

Here is one final piece of advice to those who are inclined to judge character by the mounts, or indeed by any signs on the hand or otherwise. Never judge by one sign, or you will be led into foolish mistakes. Always take the hand as a whole, for frequently some point in the formation striking you as bad may be strongly counterbalanced by other good signs. This is exceedingly important, and rightly applied it will save you many foolish pitfalls and squabbles with friends, especially in your early fortune-telling days!

The Lines of Your Destiny

We now come to the most fascinating side of palmistry—the actual study of the network of the lines upon the hand, and their relation to the mounts and to one another.

THE LIFE LINE

The Life Line starts under the Mount of Jupiter and originates from the side of the palm near the thumb and the index finger, goes around the Mount of Venus, and ultimately ends at the bracelets (the lines at the base of the palm, at the wrist). This line is seen in all human beings.

When the Life Line rises high in the hand, great ambition is shown. If you see a Life Line circling well into the palm (thus forming a large Mount of Venus), emotional characteristics such as love and generosity are shown. If, on the contrary, the line forms a small Mount of Venus, detachment will be predominant.

If the Life Line commences very feebly and gradually strengthens, this is a good sign. It indicates a weak childhood but a robust and vital maturity.

THE HEAD LINE

This line starts from the Mount of Jupiter or from above it. In most palms, the Head Line and the Life Line originate from the same place. The Head Line divides the palm into two parts. If the Head Line is broken, this may indicate some issues that have made, or will make, their effect felt upon one's thinking powers, but only if all other lines support this. An independent nature is shown when the Head Line branches off from the Life Line early in its course, and vice versa.

If the Head Line should curve toward Saturn, there is shown a materialistic outlook upon life; this is the financier's Head Line. A Head Line curving toward Apollo indicates an artistic nature, while should this line originate near Mount Jupiter, it is a sure sign of capacity for leadership, and many forceful qualities that make for success. If the

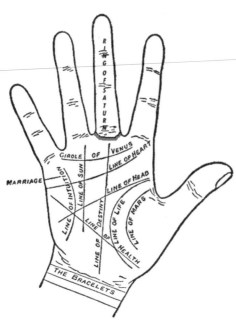

Head Line is firm, a definite, purposeful nature is probable, while a weak, wavy Head Line indicates an insecure, wavering outlook upon life.

With the Head Line joining the Heart Line, emotional qualities are to the fore; this individual is impulsive and should put the curb of reason on him- or herself. Should the Head Line have branches that run toward the Mounts of Mercury, Luna, and Mars, it is an excellent sign, showing good balance, ready wit, and quick adaptability.

THE HEART LINE

The Heart Line starts under the Mount of Mercury, reaching under the index finger and the Mount of Jupiter. When this line originates on or near the Mount of Saturn, there is a leaning toward a sensual, pleasure-loving nature. If this line rises from between Saturn and its neighbor Jupiter, we have a very deliberate, practical person, whose love, while very sincere, is governed by reason; he or she is intensely practical and rather lacking in imagination, which it would be well worth his or her while to cultivate. In this case, the head will always rule the heart, especially if the Heart Line bends toward that of the head.

Should the Heart Line cross the palm entirely, the owner is the exact opposite of the individual just mentioned. This person's heart will rule his or her head; this individual is sentimental even to a fault, and should learn to develop businesslike qualities and not be so dreamy.

A short Heart Line is a warning to take care in relationships; without this care a partnership may well come to shipwreck on a rocky shore. Forewarned is forearmed!

THE LINE OF FORTUNE

The Line of Fortune is a line running toward the Mount of Apollo. It is a valuable and somewhat rarely found line. This is the line of genius; its owner will appear to scarcely need effort; he or she will seem to fly toward success on the wings of destiny. This is the ideal, but it must be kept in mind that there are other lines that must be studied in conjunction with it.

However, its absence by no means prohibits success or makes it less likely; it merely indicates that individual effort will be required—and what is life without something to strive for?

33 Ways to Tell Your Future

THE HEALTH LINE

This line is related to health. It has no fixed starting point, but it ends at the Mount of Mercury. A good, strong Health Line is very desirable; should this line be broken, however, there is no need for alarm. It merely indicates that more attention must be paid to one's diet, exercise, and personal hygiene regimens.

THE LINE OF FATE

The Line of Fate is found in only 50 percent of the population. This line runs across the middle of the palm, from the Mount of Saturn to the bracelets, but its full course need not be traced on any particular hand. When it runs the full length of the palm, the fate of the individual may be seen as particularly lucky. Such a person has strong determination, can make quick decisions, and can be powerful without being a tyrant. He or she has the power of drawing people like a magnet, in a friendly way, and is mostly always liked.

Should the line run from the bracelets and stop at the Head Line, this is a sign that the possessor will likely have many challenging obstacles to overcome. Whether that person will surmount them depends on the strength of the Head Line. In cases where the Fate Line continues up one of the fingers, the owner must take care that success does not turn his or her head and ruin the future.

A Fate Line that wriggles its way across the palm indicates a life of ups and downs. Should the line be broken in places, it is a sign that happiness will vary from time to time. Generally speaking, if small lines run upward, out of the Fate Line, the signs are quite positive, but the reverse is the case if they run downward.

THE LINE OF MARRIAGE

The Line of Marriage is situated on the Mount of Mercury. This line is a short, comparatively inconspicuous one, found at the edge of the palm, below the little finger. It runs inward but not very far toward the center of the palm. In some hands three or four lines are found—this does not mean that these people will marry that many times. Look for the longest and deepest line. In my experience, multiple lines can mean that there could have been more than one love in this person's life, but not necessarily a romantic one. It could indicate that one or more special people, besides this person's partner, were beloved by this person and crucial in his or her life's development. In my own case, my second "marriage" line indicated the immense importance to me of Amy's late mother, the brilliant pen-and-ink artist and children's book author, Jessie Spicer Zerner.

3 Telling Fortunes with Dice

Using dice is one of the easiest ways of telling fortunes. All you need are two or three dice (you see, you were right to save that one die you found all those years ago!) and a nice even surface with a phone book or other barrier to stop the thrown dice. The method for divining what will happen in your future depends on the combination that comes up.

Method 1

Shake three dice well in a small box, and then cast once with the left hand. Add together the numbers on all three dice.

Following is a list of meanings and messages:

18: Luck does not come to you easily, but you will acquire wealth and prominence through hard labor.

17: A trip brings much happiness.

16: Your tendency is to procrastinate, which could ruin many plans and business ventures unless you overcome it.

15: Guard against a tendency to wander away from the truth. You may involve yourself needlessly in many misunderstandings and worries by this habit.

14: Lovers come to you, but your heart has not yet been captured.

13: Follow your conscience, and make amends for the misunderstanding you have caused.

12: A quick message will arrive, bringing unexpected pleasure.

11: You will meet a stranger who will prove a friend in need.

10: You have a tendency to not take a matter seriously, which may later cause regret.

9: You may count on gaining much of this world's goods and rising to a high place. You will have many friends and an interesting life.

8: Prepare for words of reproach, which you might deserve.

7: Gossip will bring sadness.

6: A marriage you hear about will astonish you.

5: A charming adventure will shortly involve you, and you will derive great joy from it.

4: Disagreeable news finds its way to you, but it is not unexpected.

3: A quarrel is followed by guilt and apologies.

Method 2

Shake two dice, and cast with the right hand. Following is a list of meanings and messages:

1 AND 1: This is the simplest kind of fortune. If you get this result, simply make any decision of importance, and it is guaranteed to come to a successful completion.

2 AND 1: If you roll this combination, be careful. You may misplace or lose something that has great sentimental value to you. The good news is that it will turn up, but it might take a while.

2 AND 2: You are about to find someone with whom you can have a long, happy relationship, so get ready.

3 AND 1: Some bad news for another can work to your benefit.

3 AND 2: If this combination comes up, do not gamble or take a business risk—be conservative.

3 AND 3: This combination signals a rivalry or seduction.

4 AND 1: Be careful with money and investments.

4 AND 2: You may be attracted to someone, and the feeling is mutual.

4 AND 3: Don't let petty things bother you. Keep the bigger picture in mind.

Dice Decisions

"He shook them up once, he shook them up twice, and staked all his luck on a throw of the dice," says an old verse, and really he might have done worse. There are many stories about people using dice because they cannot make up their mind between two plans, or, more commonly because they are more common, using a coin to help them decide. Nor is this pure chance, though it may seem to be, for, without your realizing it, your subconscious mind, which often sees further ahead than the conscious, is likely to step in and settle the matter by casting so that the right solution comes up.

Dice decisions are simple and quick. Even if you have nothing definite to settle, a throw of the dice will give you an idea of what to expect in the near future.

You will need three dice. With your left hand, put them in a box. Then create or draw an eighteen-inch circle with a pen or pencil on a paper or board, and throw the dice out onto this circle or as near it as possible. Count up the total of the numbers exposed and read according to the following list.

The meanings below apply only to such dice as fall inside the circle. If any roll outside, their number must not be included, and the rolling outside the circle foretells a quarrel, or an estrangement if the dice roll onto the floor. If one should fall on the top of another, you will receive a present.

Dice prophecies are said always to come true within nine days.

1: You are better off alone.

2: A happy partnership, perhaps even a love affair.

3: A pleasant surprise.

4: An unpleasant surprise.

5: You meet a stranger who will become your friend.

6: You will lose or have to let go of something you value.

7: Gossip will touch you and create a misunderstanding.

8: You will be justly blamed for something that has passed.

9: A wedding or celebration is near at hand.

10: A birth or new idea will prove momentous to you.

11: The ending of a friendship.

12: A communication of importance will soon arrive.

13: You will feel sensitive or hurt.

14: A new admirer is coming.

15: Take care and keep out of trouble.

16: A happy journey.

17: A profitable business.

18: Some great good is coming to you.

Telling Fortunes with Dominoes 4

Modern dominoes are usually made of wood, plastic, or metal, but in earlier sets ivory was commonly used. Standard sets in the West consist of twenty-eight rectangular tiles, also known as bones, cards, stones, or spinners. Each tile has two halves. The sides that are not blank bear dots, also called pips, numbering 1 to 6. The dots represent all the possible number combinations, from double blank to double 6.

Shuffle all of the dominoes well by laying them facedown, with the blank side up. Move them about with your hands. When they are thoroughly intermixed, draw one and find its meaning below.

DOUBLE 6s: Speculations will be successful, and your partnership will be harmonious. Happiness is coming.

6/5: Persevere in what you are doing. Success will be achieved in love and in your important plans.

6/4: A moderate income and happiness in a relationship.

6/3: A very fortunate draw for lovers; a serious relationship will be happy.

6/2: Success will bless the home of those who turn this domino; luck will be good in business. Should the desired outcome be any scheme that is underhanded or illegal, it foretells exposure; dishonesty and selfishness will not succeed.

6/1: Any young person drawing this may expect to be in love twice and will have more happiness in the second venture than in the first. For married people to draw this, it shows that good fortune is coming to them in middle life, and that if they have children, their children may seek their fortune away from them, but one child will always stay with them. If drawn by someone who is alone now, he or she is better off this way.

6/BLANK: A domino that foretells a problem or challenging situation, probably with a contract.

DOUBLE 5s: Great success in all enterprises, though it does not indicate great wealth.

5/4: A very fortunate domino to draw. Foretells a positive period in life.

5/3: A peaceful existence, not great wealth. To young people it is an indication of comfortable circumstances. It is a good prediction for people of a quiet, calm nature.

5/2: An unfortunate domino for a love situation. If a single person draws this domino, she or he will be wise to remain single for now, for marriage will not lead to happiness.

5/1: Many social enjoyments, and if a married person draws it there will be an increase in the family. As regards money, this domino portends delays.

5/BLANK: When drawn by a man, it shows a tendency in him to be mercenary and selfish, or possibly even a swindler. For a woman it is a sign to avoid falling in love too quickly to avoid disappointment. Let the woman who draws 5/2 or 5/blank remain independent.

DOUBLE 4s: This is a curious draw. For everyone who works in the open air, or with their hands, it is fortunate, but for those whose work is mental, it is an unfortunate prognostic—there may be short-term difficulties. Anyone who is giving a party will make it a great success, and possibly another big celebration will follow.

4/3: May mean marriage while still young, with a job that brings income, but a passion for a hobby that may eventually produce income. Also indicates that your secret wish will be granted.

4/2: This draw denotes considerable change. To those who have to work hard to make their living, it will be good. Change will come somehow, through an event happening either to yourself or to someone with whom you are immediately connected. A quarrel with a partner will soon be made up, and if things are unfortunate they will soon take a turn for the better.

4/1: Generally speaking, this domino means sufficient money will be available.

4/BLANK: An indication of an independent life, for now. If a female who is engaged draws this domino, she may not marry her intended: Either one or the other could prove untrustworthy. This domino is a warning to keep your own secrets; if you tell them, they will be betrayed. If a married person draws this domino, it portends a strong belief in spiritualism on the part of the conjugal partner.

DOUBLE 3s: Increased wealth. No other indication can be given.

3/2: Marriage will be happy, journeys prosperous. This draw means good fortune for lovers and also is lucky for making a big purchase.

3/1: A rather sober prediction, and everybody involved should be extremely careful with investments and gambling.

3/BLANK: To a man it foretells a wife with a temper or a flighty disposition; to a woman, it is the sign of a foolish partner; and to married people it foretells a quarrel.

DOUBLE 2s: A happy symbol, for it shows prosperity, good friends, and success.

2/1: In a business venture there are possible losses through failures unless great care is taken.

2/BLANK: To any who are dishonest, this foretells luck in their nefarious undertakings, but to respectable, honest people it denotes some kind of financial loss. For a journey, it ensures safety and a very easy recovery from a problem.

DOUBLE 1s: Shows comfortable circumstances; happiness for lovers; and fidelity in the marriage state.

DOUBLE BLANKS: This domino is favorable to the potential victims of the dishonest, for success will come to them from the discovery and avoidance of a scheme.

5 Astrology: Solar Personalities

When someone asks you, "What's your sign?" you know what the person really means is, "What is your astrology sign?" You might hear experienced astrologers such as Amy and me refer to a person's astrology sign as their "Sun sign" or "solar personality" because everyone's astrology sign is determined by which of the twelve signs of the zodiac the Sun appeared to be passing through at the moment she or he was born, as viewed from the exact spot on Earth where her or his birth occurred. The zodiac (from the Greek *kykylos zoidiakos*, meaning "circle of animals") is the narrow band of sky circling the Earth's equator through which the Sun, the Moon, and the planets appear to move when viewed by us here on Earth.

Astrology's five-thousand-year history of observing how planetary positions relate to earthly events and people has created a wealth of philosophical and psychological wisdom that, as astrologers with more than thirty years of experience, we share with you here.

Aries

The Sign of Courage

MARCH 21 TO APRIL 19

PLANET: Mars

ELEMENT: fire

QUALITY: cardinal

DAY: Tuesday

SEASON: spring

COLORS: red (all shades)

PLANTS: red poppy, thistle, ginger

PERFUME: frankincense

GEMSTONES: bloodstone, garnet, red jasper, fire opal

METAL: iron

Aries's Symbolic Meaning

The symbol for Aries is the headstrong ram. Each spring the desire to mate and stake his claim to his territory drives the ram to display his bravery by butting heads with his competitors. After a few times, the one who can handle the headache and hasn't given up is the winner. People born under the sign of Aries have a lot in common with their symbol, the ram. They are willing to butt heads with those they think are standing in their way. Sometimes, they will give up if they do not get their own way quickly enough.

Aries is considered the first sign of the zodiac. Arians, as children of Aries are called, can seem aggressive and forceful because they are trying to be independent. They like to be pioneers in some way, the first to do something. They want to do things in an original way. Even the way they are original can sometimes defy categorization. If anyone can spontaneously create a new way to be a pioneer, it is an Aries. They certainly don't like to be second or even to wait for anything for very long. They function best when they act on their first impulse and don't second-guess themselves. They hate lies and liars and can sometimes be too honest for their own good.

Aries is one of the four cardinal signs in the zodiac (the other three are Libra, Cancer, and Capricorn). These signs govern the change of season, and this makes them full of forward movement and great vitality. The cardinal signs are goal oriented, active, enthusiastic, motivated, and ambitious. They initiate change and get things moving. Those who aggressively strive to be pioneers in some way display the forceful, independent personality of the sign Aries.

Aries is also one of three fire Sun signs (like Leo and Sagittarius). People with lots of fire in their chart are active, spontaneous, enthusiastic, creative, self-sufficient, and romantic. This forceful fire element can sometimes make Arians too proud, pushy, or bossy. They act on their first impulse without any forethought and thrive when they are in charge of a project or working alone.

Like the ram, Arians are brave explorers, headstrong pioneers who always strive to seek out new experiences. Their fiery, assertive, and courageous natures are full of charm and charisma.

If you are an Aries, you express the following characteristics:

- Your thoughts and actions are independent.

- You have a commanding attitude, which makes you appear proud, yet kind and friendly.

- You are straightforward in what you have to say and direct in your opinions.

- You have a strong sense of responsibility.

- You adhere to your principles and are consistently optimistic.

- You like to participate in or be a spectator of competitive pastimes. Public speaking is a parallel or alternate hobby.

- You are sincere in your aims but impatient when they are slow in fulfillment.

Taurus
The Sign of Dependability
APRIL 20 TO MAY 20

PLANET: Venus

ELEMENT: earth

QUALITY: fixed

DAY: Friday

SEASON: spring

COLORS: spring green, blue, pink, pastels

PLANTS: daisy, magnolia, honeysuckle

PERFUME: rose

GEMSTONES: moss agate, emerald, malachite, rose quartz

METAL: copper

Taurus's Symbolic Meaning

The symbol for Taurus is the strong and determined bull. Those who can cope with anything that gets in their way display the determined, steady, and methodical personality of the sign Taurus.

People born under the sign of Taurus have a lot in common with their symbol, the bull. Though they are usually patient and gentle, when pushed too far, Taurians can become like a bull tormented by a toreador's cape. Angry or not, they are so set on their goal that they can see little or nothing else. In fact, they sometimes think they must be equally set on the way they will accomplish their mission. That can lead to stubbornness and an inability to change.

Taurians seem to be able to cope with just about anything that gets in their way. In fact, many people born under the sign of Taurus are a source of mystery and awe to their friends because no one except a Taurus will exert the energy necessary to put up with the kind of situation that everyone else would walk away from. But Taurians don't even like to walk around a situation, let alone walk away from one. Meeting challenging situations requiring patience and endurance is how they prove their abilities to themselves and those around them.

Taurus is one of the four fixed signs of the zodiac (the other three are Scorpio, Aquarius, and Leo). Fixed signs are stubborn, stable, and resolute. They have an understanding of the material world.

Taurus is also one of the three earth Sun signs (the other two are Virgo and Capricorn). The earth signs are concerned with the physical world that surrounds us—what we can see, feel, hear, and touch. Earth is a symbol of the environment, where growth takes place. The earth signs embody the concepts of nurturing, security, and protection.

Taurians get the earthly comforts they need by exerting their immense power in a sustained and methodical manner, no matter who or what tries to make them deviate from their routine. They function best when they are able to concentrate and stick to a preconceived plan, especially when they know their reward will be pleasure and luxury. While they may not be the first to jump at a new idea, once they get started they will follow it through to the finish.

If you are a Taurus, you express the following characteristics:

- Before making minor decisions, you take time to be deliberate in your thinking.
- You are proud of your endurance.
- You are devoted to your home and family.
- You like to live well.
- You prefer to depend on your own memory, which usually is infallible.
- You like wearing good apparel and costly jewelry, and enjoying first-quality food.
- You have a deep interest in music, which you like to express vocally, as an instrumentalist, or even through intense listening.

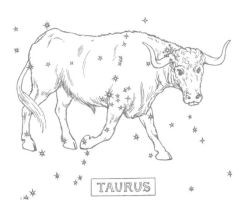

TAURUS

Gemini

The Sign of Adaptability

MAY 21 TO JUNE 20

PLANET: Mercury

ELEMENT: air

QUALITY: mutable

DAY: Wednesday

SEASON: summer

COLORS: white, yellow, multicolor

PLANTS: sweet pea, lily of the valley, mint

PERFUME: lavender

GEMSTONES: quartz crystal, tiger's eye, topaz, bicolored tourmaline

METAL: quicksilver

Gemini's Symbolic Meaning

Many thousands of years ago, the ancient sages were wise to pick as the symbol for Gemini a pair of twins. For it is as if within Geminis there are actually two different people with two different sets of values and opinions—maybe more. In fact, Geminis are legendary for functioning best when they have two or more things to do at the same time. Those born under the sign Gemini are among the best communicators of information, especially things that they have heard and their opinions. Yet, though they speak clearly and put their point across, they are often misunderstood.

Because they are interested in everything, Geminis become skilled at anything they put their lightning-quick minds to. Gemini is also the most versatile of signs. It is a rare Gemini that does only one thing extremely well. Geminis also have great dexterity. Their desire to comprehend and communicate everything quickly produces both an endless curiosity and an ability to take every side of an issue.

Gemini is one of the four mutable, or changeable, signs of the zodiac (the other three are Sagittarius, Pisces, and Virgo). Mutable signs are flexible and variable. They know how to adapt and adjust. Geminis are curious to know what life is, and they are more than willing to adjust their beliefs when information that appeals to them comes along.

Gemini has an abundance of intellectual energy. That is because Gemini is one of three astrology signs that are air signs (the other two are Aquarius and Libra). The three air signs have in common the desire for communication, freedom of expression, thought, and movement. Air is a metaphor for the invisible thoughts and ideas that motivate Gemini.

Most Geminis do not gossip any more than most people; they are just better at it and enjoy it more. You can bet that when a Gemini tells you something, it is the most up-to-date information available. Geminis love to be up on the latest things, and they try their best to know something about everything. This is the origin of stories about their legendary curiosity. Geminis think that if they only had the time and access to enough information, they could actually come to know everything.

If you are a Gemini, you express the following characteristics:

- You like to be occupied with several simultaneous pursuits.
- Advising others is one of your specialties.
- You know how to combine mental and manual aptitudes.
- Frequent change of scene is important to you.
- You prefer to do practical work, rather than concentrate on abstract theories.
- Your intellect often controls your emotions.
- You try to gain prestige through being affiliated with people of prominence.

Cancer

The Sign of Loyalty

JUNE 21 TO JULY 22

PLANET: Moon

ELEMENT: water

QUALITY: cardinal

DAY: Monday

SEASON: summer

COLORS: silver, mauve, smoke gray

PLANTS: moonflower, water lily, chamomile

PERFUME: sandalwood

GEMSTONES: moonstone, pearl, geode, hematite

METAL: silver

Cancer's Symbolic Meaning

Those born under the astrological sign Cancer are well-known for their ability to nurture others. They are especially sensitive to the ways people communicate their feelings and can be easily affected when there are bad feelings affecting those they care about. In fact, learning about feelings and the moods they produce are an important part of being a Cancerian. In astrology, the Moon is considered a planet and is associated with the sign Cancer. The Moon's ever-changing shape and its effect on the constantly shifting ocean tides is like our ever-changing moods, though the Moon's shape is a lot more predictable.

The symbol for Cancer is the crab. Feeling insecure makes them want to withdraw into their own version of a crab's protective shell. The reason why Cancerians are sometimes not as secure, sensitive, and nurturing as they wish they were is because people do not arrive in the world already an expert in the things their Sun sign is known for. They have come into this world with the challenge of the astrological sign Cancer because they want to learn how to be secure, sensitive, and nurturing.

This correlates perfectly with the fact that Cancer is one of the three water signs (the other two are Scorpio and Pisces). People with the water signs are sensitive, feeling types and are very imaginative and emotional. Cancer is the water Sun sign that is concerned with protection, caring, and comfort.

Cancer is one of the four cardinal Sun signs of astrology (the other three are Aries, Libra, and Capricorn). Cardinal signs are the first signs in each season. As such, they are initiators and act according to their aims and goals. Cancerians are legendary for their ability to nurture people and projects along, for they sense the needs of others on an emotional level. However, it is important that they remember that meeting their own emotional needs is just as important. Often, they have to be able to nurture themselves, for they are so good at nurturing others that others forget that Cancerians, too, need nurturing.

Cancerians would do well to remember that they may not be as strong as those around them think they are, but they are certainly strong enough to do what has to be done to make their dreams come true. They must resist withdrawing into their shell if they start to feel insecure. Their usual courage, patience, and gentle energy are more than they will need to make their life what they will.

If you are a Cancer, you express the following characteristics:
You have a deep reverence for tradition.

- You have an excellent memory.
- Your feelings are sensitive.
- You are tender, affectionate, and emotional.
- You are perceptive and impressionistic.
- You enjoy elaborate meals and sumptuous surroundings.
- You have a strong attachment to personal possessions and heirlooms.

Leo

The Sign of Royalty

JULY 23 TO AUGUST 22

PLANET: Sun

ELEMENT: fire

QUALITY: fixed

DAY: Sunday

SEASON: summer

COLORS: gold, orange, yellow

PLANTS: marigold, sunflower, nasturtium

PERFUME: orange blossom

GEMSTONES: amber, carnelian, citrine, topaz

METAL: gold

33 *Ways to Tell Your Future*

Leo's Symbolic Meaning

Leo is the sign of the creative organizers of the zodiac. Practically no one is as good as Leos are at recognizing the solution to a problem and organizing the means to solve it. It is this ability that gives rise to Leo's reputation as a great leader. Like all leaders, most Leos feel more comfortable when they are telling others what has to be done rather than taking care of the routine details themselves. They get annoyed with themselves for this trait, but not for long, because Leos like themselves a lot. They put themselves where there is so much that needs to be done and they associate themselves with the right group of people so that their creative input is always welcome, even if they do not always jump in and get their hands dirty.

The symbol for Leo is the strong and proud male lion, a most appropriate symbol. Not only is a group of lions referred to as a "pride," but also the importance of personal pride to those born during the time of Leo cannot be overstated. They would not want to be connected to anyone or anything that they did not feel was up to their high personal standards. This inclines Leos to provide those born under the other signs of the zodiac with a good example.

Showing us all how things are done is a special gift that Leos possess. This is why they have such a knack for drama—acting, the arts and music, or any form of display. Their generosity requires them to create situations and objects that will benefit and entertain them and those they consider worthy to be connected with them.

Leo is one of the four fixed Sun signs of astrology (the other three are Taurus, Scorpio, and Aquarius). Fixed signs are stable, resolute, and determined. They represent the force of holding steady. Being a fixed sign makes Leos loyal, stubborn, and proud. Leo is also a fire sign, one of three (Aries and Sagittarius are the other two). Fire signs are primarily energetic, enthusiastic, and impulsive.

Leos are legendary for their ability to help and protect those who acknowledge them as special people. They gain a sense of their own self-worth by giving what they think others need from them. However, it is important that they remember that they, too, need help and protection. Leos would usually be too prideful to ask for help.

If you are a Leo, you express the following characteristics:

You were born to command.

- Your attitude is dignified, but you are kind and friendly.
- You are sociable and romantic.
- You are sincere, honest, honorable, and reliable.
- You are generous and spontaneous.
- You are devoted to your family and loyal to your associates.
- You possess creative imagination and administrative aptitudes.

Virgo

The Sign of Reason

AUGUST 23 THROUGH
SEPTEMBER 22

PLANET: Mercury

ELEMENT: earth

QUALITY: mutable

DAY: Wednesday

SEASON: summer

COLORS: navy blue, gray,
green, tan

PLANTS: fern, chrysanthemum,
sage

PERFUME: patchouli

GEMSTONES: apatite,
aventurine, white opal, peridot

METAL: mercury

Virgo's Symbolic Meaning

The visual depiction of Virgo is a young woman holding shafts of wheat. While Virgo is commonly thought of as "the virgin," it is important to note that in ancient times the word *virgin* actually had two meanings: It was used not only to refer to a sexually inexperienced individual, but also to describe an independent woman who did things on her own terms and over whom no man held dominion. Indeed, Virgos thrive when they are able to do things in their own way.

The dual meaning of the word *virgin* carries over into the dual nature that most Virgos exhibit. Sometimes they are completely confident in their opinions and competence, but at other times they are as filled with self-doubt and naïveté as a young beginner. This aspect of their character correlates perfectly with the fact that Virgo is one of the four mutable, or changeable, signs of astrology (the other three being Gemini, Pisces, and Sagittarius).

The Sun passes through the mutable signs of the zodiac when we here on Earth are preparing for the change of seasons, and people born during the time of these mutable signs are therefore thought to be highly adaptable under a variety of circumstances. Flexible and open to change, such individuals deal with each situation depending on the needs and desires of the moment. Virgos are more comfortable adapting to outside influences than they are imposing their will on others.

The shafts of wheat held by the strong young woman represent Virgo's connection with the earth; this is key because Virgo is an earth sign—one of three astrological Sun signs focused on physical well-being and the practical matters of daily life (the other two earth signs are Taurus and Capricorn). The element of earth symbolizes logic, dependability, and a sense of duty to those who are considered valuable and worthy. People born during the time that the Sun is traveling through one of the three earth signs are the most reliable and responsible. They have their feet on the ground

33 Ways to Tell Your Future

and possess a practical gift for understanding the material world.

The wheat that Virgo holds is also symbolic of the harvest—the time of year during which a Virgo's birthday falls. In agrarian societies, harvesttime was the busiest and most important time of the year—hence, Virgo's hardworking tendencies.

If you are a Virgo, you express the following characteristics:

- You are neat in appearance and personal habits.
- You are proficient in performing mental and manual tasks.
- You are economical.
- You are practical in your aims.
- You prefer serious rather than hilarious companions.
- You are inclined to criticize those who are incompetent.
- You rarely are rash, hasty, or careless in your decisions or actions.

VIRGO

Astrology: Solar Personalities

Libra

The Sign of Balance

SEPTEMBER 23 TO OCTOBER 22

PLANET: Venus

ELEMENT: air

QUALITY: cardinal

DAY: Friday

SEASON: autumn

COLORS: light blue, royal blue, pastels

PLANTS: orchids, foxglove, eucalyptus

PERFUME: vanilla

GEMSTONES: diamond, jade, sapphire, blue topaz

METAL: copper

Libra's Symbolic Meaning

Libra is the only sign whose symbol is not alive, not a human, animal, or fish. Its symbol is the old-fashioned balance scale, the symbol of equal measure and justice. The scales of Libra remind us that the time of Libra was when the harvest was weighed and measured against those of other years and other farmers. Public declarations of contractual partnerships were made, and fulfilled as goods were exchanged for their fair market value. But the perfect balance of the Libran scales was also a reminder that the first six warming full Moons of the lunar year had passed and that the challenges of the next six cooling full Moons were at hand. Our ancestors knew that a balanced, loving relationship was a truly valuable commodity on those cooling nights.

Libra is one of the four cardinal Sun signs in astrology (the other three are Aries, Cancer, and Capricorn). Cardinal people like to initiate change, as each represents the beginning of a new season. Consequently, they like to take charge and to take action to direct and control. Libra is also one of the three air signs of astrology (the other two are Gemini and Aquarius). The air signs are usually connected with communication and the intellect.

The lesson for all Librans to learn is that there is an important reason why their judgment is not as refined, elegant, and accurate as they would like it to be. They have come into this world with the astrological sign Libra because they want to learn how to develop their judgment and become the best competitor for the finer things in life. Librans hate anything they consider not up to their standards and want to be surrounded by only the best. Perhaps this is why Librans are such an interesting mixture of refined judgment and fierce competitiveness.

Librans too often allow themselves to be persuaded to abandon their own judgments and distrust their intuition. It is as if they allow the scales to be put out of balance just because they cannot believe they have arrived at a perfect solution, a solution coming from within themselves. The scales that symbolize Libra are an inanimate device intended to indicate the relative weight or value of everything by attaining a position of rest, resolution, and harmony. A scale never brought to a state of equilibrium is almost worthless. Librans have a natural affinity with the unseen, intuitive side of life. With the exceedingly rare and keen perception characteristic of the sign Libra, there is no human attainment beyond their grasp.

If you are a Libra, you express the following characteristics:

- You are well-balanced mentally and emotionally.
- You are interested in humanitarian causes.
- You are motivated by goodwill toward others.
- You love art in all its forms.
- You are sincere and idealistic.
- You have a cheerful disposition.
- You are congenial and courteous.

LIBRA

Scorpio

The Sign of Resourcefulness

OCTOBER 23 TO NOVEMBER 21

PLANET: Pluto

ELEMENT: water

QUALITY: fixed

DAY: Tuesday

SEASON: autumn

COLORS: black, dark red, maroon

PLANTS: gardenia, rhododendron, anemone

PERFUME: tuberose

GEMSTONES: agate, onyx, ruby, black opal

METAL: plutonium

Scorpio's Symbolic Meaning

Scorpio is the master detective of the zodiac. If there's something or someone Scorpios want to know about, there is nothing and no one who can prevent them from discovering the hidden truth. It is as if they feel compelled to know all the secrets just in case they need to use them to prove how powerful they are.

When it comes to their own secrets, Scorpios are equally skilled at keeping them from others. In this way they prevent others from having power over them. They rarely volunteer information, for the same reason. Power in all its forms is one of the biggest issues for Scorpios to deal with. Most of them are powerful and know it. However, if Scorpios doubt their own power, they become so attracted to power that they are willing to do practically anything to get it. This can obviously put them in intense situations.

Most Scorpios are as fearless as their most well-known symbol, the scorpion. But like a scorpion, they can be so intent on stinging something that they end up stinging themselves. Their intensity is such that other people can't believe that they really mean what they are saying. Scorpios are often misunderstood because of the intensity of their passion.

Scorpio is one of the four fixed Sun Signs in astrology (the other three are Taurus, Aquarius, and Leo). Fixed signs are associated with stability and determination. Concentration, focus, consolidation, and perseverance are all hallmarks of a fixed Sun sign. Scorpio is the fixed water sign of the zodiac. It is one of three water signs in the zodiac (the other two are Pisces and Cancer). Water is the element that makes a Scorpio emotional, sensitive, feeling, and hidden. In the case of Scorpio, still waters do run deep.

The lesson for Scorpios to learn is that there is an important reason why their life does not provide them with as many peak experiences as they would like. They have come into this world with the astrological sign Scorpio because they want to learn how to develop their ability to work their powerful will on the world. The sign Scorpio rules magic, and Scorpios want to make big changes in their lives, the kinds that appear to other people as almost magical transformations.

If you are a Scorpio, you express the following characteristics:

- You are self-reliant and forceful.
- You can be reserved, secretive, and skeptical.
- You possess considerable perseverance.
- You are devoted to your loved ones.
- You are willing to make personal sacrifices for those you hold in high esteem.
- Your determination to do as you please is dominant.
- You are idealistic as well as practical in your viewpoints.

Sagittarius

The Sign of Action

NOVEMBER 23 TO DECEMBER 22

PLANET: Jupiter

ELEMENT: fire

QUALITY: mutable

DAY: Thursday

SEASON: autumn

COLORS: purple (all shades)

PLANTS: hydrangea, saffron, rosemary

PERFUME: peony

GEMSTONES: amethyst, sodalite, sugilite, tanzanite

METAL: pewter

Sagittarius's Symbolic Meaning

The symbol for Sagittarius is Chiron, the bow-wielding centaur—half man and half horse. In Greek mythology, Chiron the centaur was the first doctor of herbal medicine, a wise sage, and he was the teacher of the great warrior Achilles.

The legend of Chiron may have started out with stories of a wise and skillful hunter, perhaps the leader of the first tribe to hunt on horseback. The other tribes might have seen them as being half man and half horse. Travel on horseback made it possible for people to see many different places and tribes, with all kinds of unique customs. When they returned from their journeys, they kept their own tribes hypnotized with stories of these far-off lands.

Those born under the sign of Sagittarius share this love of travel, animals—especially horses—the great outdoors, natural healing, and all things foreign. They are the philosopher-teachers of the

zodiac, and without Sagittarians performing this vital function, each generation would be forced to start from scratch without the accumulated wisdom of the ages to guide them. Not only do Sagittarians keep the torch of learning alive, but they also actively seek out knowledge and the wisdom to use it properly. They are interested only in the ultimate truth, because any other truth would not be worth knowing and teaching to others.

This is why Sagittarians have such a reputation for being blunt. Sagittarians feel that anyone who is telling the truth should be able to defend his or her position against any question, even if the question is totally tactless and without regard for social customs. Sagittarians are in a hurry and want to keep traveling, learning, and spreading what they've learned. They don't have time to waste beating around the bush. Never expect them to apologize for having annoyed someone when they were only trying to get at the truth.

If you are a Sagittarius, you express the following characteristics:

- You are gifted with high ethics.
- You are motivated by goodwill toward others.
- You are idealistic about your work.
- You are tolerant and considerate.
- You are loyal in love and friendship.
- You refrain from interfering with others.
- You are philanthropic and philosophical.

Capricorn

The Sign of Authority

DECEMBER 22 TO JANUARY 19

PLANET: Saturn

ELEMENT: earth

QUALITY: cardinal

DAY: Saturday

SEASON: winter

COLORS: black, dark brown, gray

PLANTS: pansy, ivy, tulip, lilac

PERFUME: vetivert

GEMSTONES: jet, obsidian, smoky quartz, turquoise

METAL: lead

Capricorn's Symbolic Meaning

A mountain goat is the symbol for the sign Capricorn. The mountain goat is tireless as it makes its way to the top of mountain after mountain. Most Capricorns are equally tireless in their efforts to get to the top of their respective professions. Most people might think that Capricorns desire above all to attain the respect of the masses. It is more accurate to say that they crave the respect of those whom they, themselves, respect. This is as important to them as is living in wealth and style, yet another way they gain the respect of the in-crowd.

To get to the top, Capricorns are willing to do what is expected of them. This gets them the reputation of being conservative, when deep inside, they are quite sensual. They are conservative in the best sense of the word. You conserve what you have so that you will have enough when you need it. This is true practicality. Capricorns make wonderful executives. In fact, it is difficult for them to show their true worth until they are left alone to assume some kind of definite responsibility. Once they feel this weight resting on their shoulders and realize that the success of a venture is up to them, they will rise to the occasion, succeeding where others would give up. Once they make something of themselves, they display a kind of energy that can overcome almost any obstacle.

Capricorns have this personality trait because their sign is one of the four cardinal Sun signs in astrology (the other three are Aries, Libra, and Cancer). Cardinal signs approach life with a great deal of drive. They are enterprising; they love to be on the go and initiate new activities. They accomplish their goals. Capricorn is also one of the three earth Sun signs in astrology (the other two are Taurus and Virgo). Earth signs respond to the world through their five senses: what they see, hear, taste, touch, and smell. This earth-element energy gives Capricorns patience, discipline, and a great understanding about how the world works.

Their awareness of how far they have to go to achieve the respect they crave can sometimes get to Capricorns and make them pessimistic or, less often, depressed. This tendency actually comes not from the realization of how far they have to go, but from the fact that they will rarely allow themselves to become inspired and energized by what they have already accomplished. Though they may not see it as well as those around them do, they have, from a young age, already accomplished many things that would be sufficient to delight those who are not Capricorns.

If you are a Capricorn, you express the following characteristics:

- You are practical, logical, serious, and conservative.
- You have genuine respect for time and property.
- You are ambitious and resourceful.
- You strive for personal and business eminence.
- You are efficient and dependable.
- You have a copious sense of humor.
- You possess executive skill.

Aquarius

The Sign of Progress

JANUARY 20 TO FEBRUARY 18

PLANET: Uranus

ELEMENT: air

QUALITY: fixed

DAY: Saturday

SEASON: winter

COLORS: electric blue, sky blue, ultraviolet

PLANTS: tiger lily, bird of paradise, parsley

PERFUME: lemon verbena

GEMSTONES: rock crystal, fluorite, azurite, lapis lazuli

METAL: uranium

Aquarius's Symbolic Meaning

The symbol of the sign Aquarius is the water bearer pouring out his bounty to quench the thirst of world. For this reason, many people mistakenly think Aquarius is a water sign. Water was the element the ancient sages connected with the realm of emotion, empathy, and intuition. However, Aquarius is not a water sign. The element associated with Aquarius is air, the realm of ideas. People born under the sign Aquarius like to think in broad and theoretical terms, and they want to "pour out" their ideas to quench the thirst of the world.

Being mistaken for a water sign is a very significant clue to the lesson for Aquarians. Water symbolizes emotions and empathy, and Aquarians are often perceived to be lacking in both. Aquarians, being concerned for the good of all, are inspired to invent solutions to society's problems. To do this requires a freethinking mind, unfettered by tradition or fear of disturbing the status quo. They are the mad scientists and absentminded professors of the zodiac. Aquarians learn from the past to change what they find distasteful in the present, for by doing that they create the future they envision.

The emotional detachment necessary to see society's problems clearly and to try to solve those problems—without regard to the ramifications of the actions necessary to make these sometimes drastic changes—make Aquarians seem to lack empathy for individual hardship. Aquarians should examine actions they plan to take to make sure they will not be hurtful to others, even if that is not their intent.

Aquarius is one of the four fixed Sun signs in astrology (the other three are Taurus, Leo, and Scorpio). Fixed signs are concentrated, stubborn, and persistent. They are the ones who provide the stability to see things through. Aquarius is also one of the three air Sun signs in astrology (the other two are Libra and Gemini). Air represents the mind, ideas, and the ability to think; Aquarian ideas may be unusual or even original, but once formed, they tend to remain fixed. Aquarians refuse to budge whenever an issue involves what they believe to be a matter of principle.

Once the scientific mind of an Aquarian is finished thinking about a subject theoretically, he or she returns to the world of emotions. In fact, Aquarians can easily feel themselves being overcome by feelings of empathy for those less fortunate. This is what inspires them in the first place to come up with solutions to society's urgent problems.

If you are an Aquarius, you express the following characteristics:

- You are friendly and good-natured.
- You are liberal in your opinions and beliefs.
- You strive for knowledge.
- You are interested in unusual occupations and professions.
- Your ideas are imaginative, inventive, and original.
- Your happiness is derived from inspiring others.
- You are deeply interested in modern methods and progressive trends.

Pisces

The Sign of Perception

FEBRUARY 19 TO MARCH 20

PLANET: Neptune

ELEMENT: water

QUALITY: mutable

DAY: Thursday

SEASON: winter

COLORS: lavender, sea green, aqua

PLANTS: wisteria, gardenia, lotus

PERFUME: ylang-ylang

GEMSTONES: aquamarine, coral, mother of pearl, pearl

METAL: tin

Pisces's Symbolic Meaning

Pisces is the last sign of the zodiac. Because it is the last of the twelve signs, it contains a bit of all of them. Pisceans are so sensitive to the feelings of other people that they can sometimes experience as their own the strong feelings of those around them without realizing it. This explains why Pisceans are so easily able to understand how other people are feeling.

In fact, Pisceans are so sensitive to the feelings of others that it is not good for them to be near people who are angry, sad, or disturbed. Sometimes, it is hard for those born during the time of Pisces to understand why they are feeling the way they are. If they are in conflict with themselves, as the Piscean symbol suggests—two fish locked in tension, forever pulling each other in opposite directions—this can represent the personality whose inner self is always preparing to retreat from the world.

Pisces is associated with both empathy and telepathy. This natural ability to be invisibly connected to those around them and those around the world is both the blessing and the curse of all Pisceans. It enables them to feel exactly how to help those they care about, which is a Piscean specialty. It is exhausting and hard on Pisceans' emotions, however, to have other people's lives intrude so on their own.

Pisces is one of the four mutable Sun signs in astrology (the other three are Gemini, Virgo, and Sagittarius). Mutable signs are able to adapt and adjust. Pisces is also one of the three water Sun signs in the zodiac (the other two are Scorpio and Cancer). Water signs value their emotions and their intuition.

When they turn their sensitivity to the real world, Pisceans have the capacity to make substantial amounts of money in business ventures. If you think that seems unlikely given Pisces' reputation for dreaminess and escapism, remember that as the last sign, Pisces contains a bit of all the other ones. Pisceans are most aware of both the things that unite us all and the immense differences between people. This is one of their great strengths, but if they let themselves be totally ruled by their emotions or let the sorrow of the human condition push them to escapist behavior, it can turn into a great weakness. When they learn to balance their innate intuitive skills with a logical approach that does not ignore what is real but unpleasant, they can accomplish great things.

If you are a Pisces, you express the following characteristics:

- You are impressionistic and perceptive.
- You try to maintain an aura of peace and harmony around you.
- You enjoy meditating.
- You are sympathetic and compassionate.
- You are kind and philanthropic.
- You are religious as well as fatalistic in viewpoint.
- You know how to keep secrets that are entrusted to you.

Face Fortunes

A knowledge of face reading can be helpful to everyone in social as well as business affairs. It is useful to be able to read a face, to tell from its general contour and specific features the type of individual you are... well, facing. Face reading offers an explanation for the many sometimes immediate likes and dislikes we get about people. It goes beyond their tendencies and those peculiar characteristics that make them different from others.

Knowing face reading, even its elementals, can help you strip a person you are reading of superficial mannerisms and traits so you can read his or her true nature and temperament. Knowing the character of the man or woman you deal with, the person you fancy, or a friend whose actions baffle you can be a tremendous help and safeguard in all relationships.

It is important to realize that facial surgery for cosmetic reasons can have an effect on one's personality, a word taken from the Greek word *persona*, meaning mask. Therefore, within reason, you can read those who have had it as if they were born the way they look now. Never, however, do face reading on any body part that has been severely injured or that has any medical conditions. Remember, also, that you should never judge a person by his or her face or any one trait; you have to take all things about the person, including his or her behavior, into consideration before rendering your judgment.

The Art of Face Reading

Forehead

A large forehead indicates intelligence; a narrow one, an unconvincing mind. Should it project, it indicates avarice and love of gain. A depressed forehead announces the worst passions and insensitivity; a smooth forehead is a sign of small talents; a wrinkled forehead indicates care or deliberation.

Eyes

Eyes handsome, vivid, open, brilliant, announce noble instincts. Blue eyes are an indication of intelligence; brown, of force of mind; green eyes often indicate an indomitable spirit. Small eyes denote ardent passions; dull eyes, brutishness; liquid eyes denote a delicate disposition; persons squinting are either in need of corrective lenses or, as face reading traditionally interprets it, full of bad faith; those who stare as children do are naturally childish and amiable. Eyes large and limpid are a sign of kindness.

Nose

A large nose, enlarged at the base, can indicate intelligence, discretion, and love of work. A large nose, turned up, can designate a bold person, always seeking pleasure. A large and long nose can announce prudence; a nose long and thin, frivolity and courage. A very flat nose often signifies self-indulgence (or a boxer!). An aquiline nose, slightly prominent, is usually a sign of pride. A pointed nose, with piercing eyes, can denote a sarcastic disposition. A pointed nose, with thin lips, often marks acquisitiveness. A red nose is often the sign of excess or the intense form of acne called rosacea.

Mouth

A well-balanced mouth is usually a sign of good character. A small mouth often announces timidity and discretion. A very large mouth can indicate deceptive tendencies.

Lips

Thick lips can be an indication of innate goodness. Thin lips announce a love of good work; if they accompany a large mouth, gossip may be a problem. Sensual persons often have long lips and large mouths. When one lip is more advanced than the other, judgment could be slow or the person without humor.

Ears

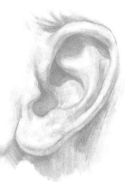

Large ears can indicate pride and anger. Small ears, well curved, often denote cleverness. Very small ears are known to indicate one who holds back. Ears long and narrow may denote a jealous tendency. Flat ears are often found to be a sign of procrastination.

Chin

A large and fleshy chin sometimes announces bad taste or lack of decorum. A flat chin can indicate someone who doesn't mind acting disagreeably. A very long chin is often the sign of pride. A cleft chin usually announces cheerfulness.

Voice

A voice deep and strong usually announces a robust person, daring and a great talker. A deadened voice often indicates timidity born of hard times. A rich, full, clear voice is said to be a sign of intelligence. A trembling voice can indicate that the person is dealing with fear or envy. A loud voice often denotes courage. A rough, annoying voice marks an unenlightened mind that cares not at all for others.

7 Phrenology: Head Reading

What Do Your Bumps Mean?

Just feel the shape of your own head, and then ask a friend to let you do the same thing to him or her. Most likely you will be very surprised at the difference between the two. You may have bumps or raised areas in certain places, while your friend has them in totally different parts.

The practice of phrenology (from the Greek *phrenos*, meaning "mind" and *logos*, meaning "logic"), which is the reading of bumps on the head, was developed in 1796 by Franz Joseph Gall, a German physician. He postulated that the shape of various areas of the skull, raised areas and bumps in certain places, corresponded to certain mental characteristics. Phrenology became very popular during the nineteenth century, so much so that it was thought that if you had bumps in certain places, you must have the corresponding characteristics, and if you did not have them, then you could not have those qualities.

Phrenology is a technique that can be easily learned. Of course, there is much to learn, but there is no need to know a great deal about it if you merely want to assess a person's character in general terms. As we said in the introduction to this book, character is destiny.

A chart is supplied on the following page, and on it is marked out just enough to enable you to read a head with ease. Only certain areas are mapped out; the rest of the head may also have bumps, but these bumps are not relevant at this point in our study. The areas are as follows:

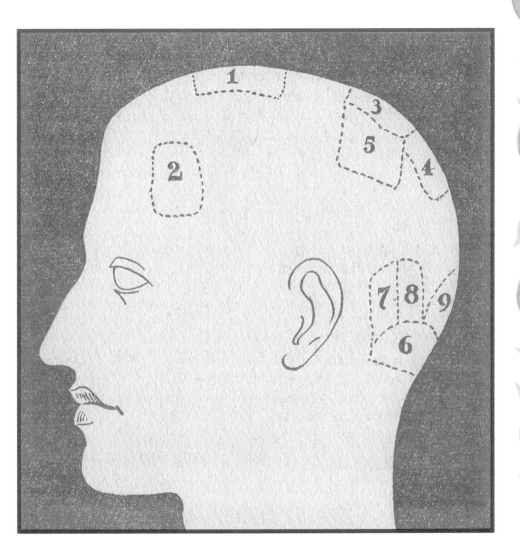

Area 1

Lying at the top of the head, in the center and coming a little way toward the forehead:

If this area is well developed—raised a bit from its surrounding areas or possessing one or two bumps—it shows that the individual has a benevolent nature. He or she is generous and kind and will work for the good of others and not think only of him or herself. If the area is overdeveloped—raised too high or possessing more than two bumps—the individual will be inclined to favor others at the expense of his or her own safety; if it is underdeveloped—if there is a depression there or no bumps at all—he or she will have to watch a tendency to be cruel and selfish.

Area 2

Situated above but a little behind the eye; usually the area is just covered by hair:

When this area is well developed, it shows that the individual possesses plenty of happiness and a good sense of humor. He or she is a pleasant person, smiles on adversity, and is excellent company. If the area is overdeveloped, the individual is one who can never be taken seriously, who pokes fun at everything; if it is underdeveloped, he or she is the type of person who is never known to smile.

Area 3

In the middle of the head, where it curves down toward the back of the neck:

In cases where this area is well developed, the person is one who has strength of mind; he or she is firm with actions; cannot be persuaded against his or her own judgment; and likes his or her own way. If this area is overdeveloped, the person is obstinate and stubborn; if it is underdeveloped, he or she is easily led, is apt to waver, and has not a mind of his or her own.

Area 4

In the middle of the head, lower down the back than Area 3:

When this area is found in a well-developed condition, the possessor is a person who has dignity, self-esteem, and proper pride. He or she is one who lives an upright life, because he or she puts a high price on these qualities. If this area is overdeveloped, the individual is overconfident—he or she is too egotistical and haughty; if it lacks development, he or she is too humble and suffers from an inferiority complex.

Area 5

Lying beside area 3 and area 4:

To find this area well developed is a sure sign that the possessor is a conscientious individual; it shows that he or she has a high sense of duty, and life will center around actions that are based on what he or she thinks is right. If this area is overdeveloped, the possessor will never progress far because he or she will always be stopping and wondering whether what he or she proposes to do is right; if it is underdeveloped, the possessor is one who does not care whether what he or she does is right or wrong, so long as it brings pleasure and gain.

Area 6

At the base of the skull, at the back, where it joins the backbone:

If this area is well developed, it shows that the individual has the power of loving somebody in a fulfilling manner. He or she will fall in love when a suitable occasion arises and will make an excellent partner.

Area 7

A slight distance away from the back of the ear:

When this area is well developed, the individual may be counted on to be courageously inclined. He or she will not know the meaning of fear and will not hold back because troubles may be brewing. If this area is overdeveloped, we have a quarrelsome person, and if it is underdeveloped, the person is one who is afraid of his or her own shadow.

Area 8

Beside Area 7, but more in the center of the back of the head:

Whenever this area is properly developed, it shows that the possessor would make an admirable husband or wife. He or she would be devoted, loyal, and attentive. If the area is overdeveloped, the possessor has a jealous disposition; if it is underdeveloped, he or she is fickle and apt to flirt with others.

Area 9

Beside Area 8, in the center of the back of the head, low down:

Should this area be well developed, it shows that the possessor has a proper love and regard for children and that he or she thinks no person has experienced the fullest joys of life who has not become a parent. If this area is overdeveloped, the possessor thinks so much of children that he or she spoils them; if it is underdeveloped, he or she is of the type that does not make having children a priority.

Chart of Phrenology

1: Benevolence, Generosity, Kindness

2: Happiness, Wit, Mirth

3: Firmness, Strength of Mind

4: Self-Esteem, Dignity, Pride

5: Conscientiousness, Sense of Duty

6: Love

7: Courage

8: Desire for Partnership

9: Love of Children

Reading Body Language

If possible, use a straight-back chair with no arms. Ask your subject to take a seat. Notice the first position he or she takes. Here are character readings for the most common positions people take.

BOLT UPRIGHT: When people take this position, it shows that they are always on the alert. They have a good business sense and can drive a very hard bargain if the occasion arises. They always remember their dignity and are afraid they will be the subject of gossip.

FEET CROSSED: People who sit with their feet crossed at the ankles and arms akimbo are individuals who take a broad view of life. They have an indulgent eye to the young. These people can be counted on in times of trouble to be there with hopeful and cheery counsel. They should avoid being too easygoing, or unscrupulous people may take advantage of them and bring trouble.

HANDS ON KNEES AND FEET APART: These individuals are quite pleased with themselves and are quite content to view the world from their own angle and not heed other people. These people should try to cultivate a wider outlook. If they conquer a stubborn tendency, life should hold many pleasant surprises. If not, they may find that friends want to drop them. They should remember that people are sensitive and can be led better than driven.

KNEES CROSSED: Individuals who sit with their legs crossed at the knees take a kind and tolerant view of life. They will always be popular, for they put themselves out often to help other people over rough patches. These individuals' one fault is that they are inclined to put pleasure before work.

ON THE EDGE OF THE SEAT: People who sit on the edge of the chair are nervy individuals. They are afraid to be late and can never rest. These people will always get on in life, but they run the danger of losing all the fun because of a fear of not doing their best at work. These individuals have a conscientious nature. They will never have many friends, because people won't take the trouble to get to know them. Those who do know them will respect them, however.

ONE FOOT FORWARD AND ONE FOOT BACK: People who sit like this are ever ready to seize an opportunity, but in an eagerness to get things done, they are inclined to be slapdash. They should try to get a grip on themselves, and success will follow. These individuals will always be popular and are sure to choose good partners.

HANDS IN POCKETS: If people sit like this, you can be sure they are of a calm, not easily perturbed nature. Life will flow by, and unless it affects them personally, these individuals won't be stirred too much by events. They have a strong tendency to play tricks on their friends and should take care that they do not make enemies by fooling around.

SIDEWAYS: People who sit this way do not bother themselves too much about conversation. If they want to do anything very much, they will, no matter what anyone says. Friends will always flock around. These people should be careful not to spend money recklessly, or this habit may create some slight difficulty. They will be in a happy relationship.

HANDS ON BUT NOT IN POCKETS: This attitude is one that shows a genial nature. You can always count on these people having a good sense of humor. When children are around, you are almost certain to see these people handing out money or presents to them. These individuals are inclined to be indolent and easily put off a project that means extra work. They should try to conquer this fault. They should avoid being alone too much, or they will get morose.

LOLLING BACK: These people are of a happy-go-lucky nature. They like comfort above all things, and you won't find them going out on a cold night unless absolutely forced to! Their intentions are good, but sometimes they lack the effort to carry them out. They will get on much better if they try to assert themselves more. These individuals could easily be a force to be reckoned with if they cared.

LEANING FORWARD, HANDS BETWEEN KNEES: People who sit like this are of an eager nature. They like to miss nothing of what's going on, and are ever ready to spring to attention at the slightest warning. They should avoid getting too serious and should try to force themselves to go out in company more. These individuals will have a fatal fascination for romance, but they do not as a rule hold much interest for long.

FEET STRETCHED STRAIGHT IN FRONT: Here are people who like to take life as it comes. They will take the ups and downs quite calmly and never grumble. Older people will like them very much,

because they are patient with them. They should get on quite well, for their nature is an adaptable one. These individuals should always be sure to get plenty of exercise.

ASTRIDE CHAIR: This attitude is one that belongs to people with a love of company and a happy nature. They like to see all that is going on and always want to be in the thick of things. They will have friends wherever they go. They take a broad outlook on life and can see both sides of a question. These individuals should do well in almost any job, as long as they are happy. They will have no difficulty in picking a life mate when the time comes.

HANDS BEHIND HEAD: People who sit with hands clasped at the back of the head have a lazy streak, although they can usually keep it well in check. It takes a good lot to rouse their temper, but once they get going, they can be very angry. They will be moderately successful in life. These individuals should marry someone who will urge them on rather than one who worships blindly.

FEET RESTING SIDEWAYS: Individuals who sit with their feet resting on their sides are inclined to be bashful. They do not like to push themselves forward but should try to force themselves to do so. In short, these people are inclined to have an inferiority complex and should try at all costs to conquer it. If they do so, they should get on quite well, for many people like them. They are not good mixers, but in spite of that they should go out a lot.

Reading Tarot Cards

The One-Card Technique

Each card of the Tarot embodies a very specific concept and psychology, and any one card can be selected as an answer to a question or as a meditative tool. Use the one-card technique as a daily guide to your day's activities. If you find a special affinity with the Tarot, you may want to consider obtaining our *Tarot Discovery Kit*, which is designed to further your skills.

Shuffling the cards of the Tarot at the same moment you are concentrating on your question causes your question and the cards you select in answer to your question to be linked together by the power of your intention and concentration. Your state of mind as you shuffle, cut, and draw your card implies a future course of events in regard to the situation you are asking about. They are connected in a meaningful way because they are happening at the same time.

By shuffling and selecting one card from your chosen Tarot deck as you calmly and sincerely ask for advice about your situation, we believe that you cause your Higher Self to guide you to select the proper card. Each Tarot card that you choose symbolizes and reflects a particular energy. Your Tarot reading will offer you a perspective on the situation you are inquiring about. When using the one-card technique, if a single card falls from the deck while you are shuffling, you need look no further—that card is your answer.

Always say your question as you shuffle the cards, either to yourself or out loud. There is no right or wrong way to shuffle; just do it in a manner that feels comfortable to you. Here are some suggested ways in which you can phrase your one-card questions:

1. Give me a message about _____ for my highest good and greatest joy.

2. Give me guidance and insight about _____.

3. What do I need to know about _____?

4. What is the meaning of _____?

5. What is the lesson or purpose of _____?

6. How am I perceived by _____?

7. What is going to be the future outcome of _____ if the present course is / is not changed?

8. How can I improve _____?

The Major Arcana

THE FOOL: Have fun—you are truly blessed!

THE MAGICIAN: You've got the power and the skill to make magic.

HIGH PRIESTESS: Use your intuition—you know the answer.

THE EMPRESS: Welcome a time of creativity, fertility, and peace.

THE EMPEROR: Develop the ability to see things more clearly.

THE HIEROPHANT: Relax; you're being too rigid and dogmatic.

THE LOVERS: This is a good time for romance; find an equal partner.

THE CHARIOT: Take control of your life, and drive forward.

STRENGTH: More can be accomplished through gentleness than through brutality.

THE HERMIT: Guidance from a wise person, teacher, or book is indicated.

WHEEL OF FORTUNE: Take a chance, for luck is with you.

JUSTICE: You are about to get exactly what you deserve, so be prepared.

33 *Ways to Tell Your Future*

THE HANGED MAN: You're in a rut; add more excitement to your life and experiment.

DEATH: Every end is a new beginning—let go.

TEMPERANCE: Develop patience; nothing can be gained now by rushing or forcing.

THE DEVIL: You're being held prisoner by your own demons; take time for a spiritual cleansing.

THE TOWER: A shocking turn of events creates a powerful learning experience.

THE STAR: Open up to the inspiration and illumination that surrounds you; try to meditate.

THE MOON: Moodiness is indicated. Use your feelings to guide you through the unknown.

THE SUN: Happiness, vitality, and good health are all around you.

JUDGMENT: This is perfect time to act, so don't hesitate.

THE WORLD: Completion and fulfillment are at hand. You are whole.

Wands

ACE: This indicates the beginning of something with great potential for growth and development.

2: Make plans to embark on an enterprise; make a list.

3: Opportunities are around you.

4: Harmony and stability are indicated.

5: Compete and play to win.

6: Victory can be yours. Enjoy the applause.

7: You may achieve success against incredible odds.

8: This indicates great haste, great hope, and messages of love.

9: Be prepared and disciplined: you have strength in reserve.

10: You are carrying a heavy burden; struggle is indicated.

PAGE: This indicates a verbal, uninhibited person.

KNIGHT: This indicates an impetuous, impassioned person.

QUEEN: This indicates an active, energetic, goal-oriented woman.

KING: This indicates an action-oriented man, a good leader.

Swords

ACE: This indicates a triumph of power and great concentration.

2: Open your eyes and confront the problem.

3: A broken heart is indicated.

4: Hibernate and rest before a new effort.

5: Conquer or be conquered.

6: This shows movement away from present difficulties.

7: This indicates trickery or a plan that may fail.

8: You may be trapped by indecision and procrastination.

9: Anxiety and sleep problems are indicated.

10: You have been through a painful experience.

PAGE: One who is a communicator is indicated.

KNIGHT: This indicates a brave and dominating, active person.

QUEEN: This indicates an ambitious, temperamental, and truthful woman.

KING: This indicates a forceful, but diplomatic, authoritarian man.

Cups

ACE: You will experience the beginning of true emotional satisfaction.

2: This shows an equal exchange between lovers or friends.

3: Celebrate with light-heartedness.

4: Reevaluate your goals.

5: This indicates feelings of failure; it may indicate a breakup.

6: Enjoy a return to the simple pleasures of childhood.

7: This indicates illusory success and castles in the sky.

8: Success may be abandoned as soon as it's achieved.

9: This is the wish card—your wish will come true.

10: This indicates perfect domestic bliss and success.

PAGE: Playfulness, affection, and dreaminess are indicated.

KNIGHT: The consummate romantic is shown.

QUEEN: A nurturing, generous woman is shown.

KING: An emotionally sensitive, giving man is shown.

Pentacles

ACE: This is the beginning something with great potential for material success.

2: Juggle two things gracefully, and multitask.

3: This card means work shared in a fortunate way.

4: You may be assured material gain, so don't be stingy, and be a good manager.

5: Distress and anxiety are indicated—you are trying to find the way back home.

6: Charity freely dispensed will be rewarded.

7: Take a pause during the development of a project.

8: This indicates perfectionism, and the master artisan.

9: You will experience independence and enjoyment of the good things in life.

10: Protection and perfect financial success can be yours.

PAGE: This indicates respect for learning and new ideas, and a message about money.

KNIGHT: A responsible, trustworthy workingman is shown.

QUEEN: An earthy, practical, well-to-do woman is shown.

KING: This indicates a reliable, worldly, successful man.

IO Dowsing: Using a Pendulum

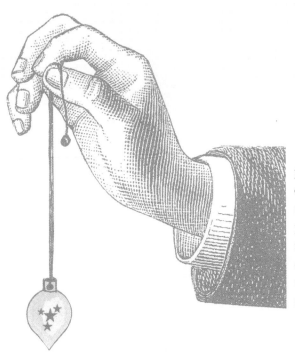

Most people know what a pendulum is—it's a weight, light or heavy, hanging at the bottom of a rope or chain, like the weights you can see hanging on the ends of the chains in genuine grandfather clocks—but fewer people know what is meant by using a pendulum for the purpose of dowsing.

What Is Dowsing?

Dowsing is most commonly known as a tool for finding water. You may have seen it done on television or in movies, or if you live in the country, you may have seen a dowser plying her or his craft in person. A person, known as the dowser, stands holding the arms of a forked tree branch in his or her hands until the single section of the branch starts to point down to the ground, sometimes pulling the dowser down until the branch touches the ground. At this point, the dowser usually looks up and says, "There's water below me—dig your well here!" Sometimes the dowser uses two thin pieces of wire bent at right angles so they can be held lightly and allowed to swing back and forth. When they cross, water is below.

You may think that dowsing is a quaint, superstitious practice from the past, but if you ask around, you will find that many communities have a water dowser or "diviner" who is called upon when a new well

is being dug or drilled. Dowsing is also used in the search for oil and for minerals and ore deposits, and in the practice of holistic healing for guidance in diagnosis and treatment. There is a long tradition of pendulum dowsers helping to find missing objects such as pets and jewelry—something that we have done quite a few times for friends—and even missing people and lost archeological sites. Many utility companies use dowsing when searching for buried pipes and cables.

Dowsing is an intuitive discipline. It demands that one remain both alert rationally and open intuitively. In our years of research, we have determined that this is the same state of relaxed awareness that enables psychics and practitioners of Tarot, astrology, and other divinatory arts to make accurate predictions. The brain-wave activity of dowsers shows a very high degree of left- and right-brain integration as well as simultaneous brain-wave activity at all levels. Similar results are also seen in those

practicing other intuitive disciplines such as ESP, reading Tarot cards, or doing other kinds of energy readings such as hands-on healing and aura work. This is the optimum state of mind in which to absorb knowledge and, if you are lucky, wisdom.

Dowsing thus empowers us all in the exploration of our own inner environment as well as in our outer environment. As within, so without—as above, so below. This is the first law of the metaphysical (beyond the physical) approach to living your life in harmony with nature—the outer world—and with the inner world of your true spiritual nature. Dowsing is a unique and important tool for spiritual growth and the development of our mind-body connection. It also accelerates and guides the practitioner along his or her spiritual path and helps to place the seeker outwardly at the optimum spot for him or her in life's progression.

After many years and thousands of readings, we have come to believe beyond doubt

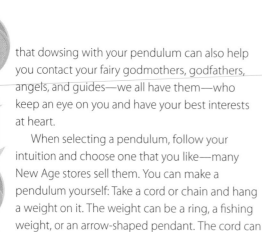

that dowsing with your pendulum can also help you contact your fairy godmothers, godfathers, angels, and guides—we all have them—who keep an eye on you and have your best interests at heart.

When selecting a pendulum, follow your intuition and choose one that you like—many New Age stores sell them. You can make a pendulum yourself: Take a cord or chain and hang a weight on it. The weight can be a ring, a fishing weight, or an arrow-shaped pendant. The cord can be four to ten inches long.

How does dowsing work? The word *radiesthesia* is used to describe the paranormal or parapsychological ability to detect radiation of subtle energy (not nuclear radiation) within the human body. According to the theory, all human bodies give off unique or characteristic radiations, as do all other physical bodies or objects. Such radiations are often termed an "aura."

A practitioner of radiesthesia believes in his or her ability to detect the interplay of these radiations. Thus, radiesthesia is cited as the explanation for such phenomena as dowsing by pendulums, as in our *Truth Fairy* pendulum kit; automatic writing, as in our *Ghostwriter Automatic Writing Kit*; and talking boards, such as our *Enchanted Spellboard*.

Form Your Question: What Do You Want to Know?

For thousands of years, pendulum dowsing has enabled people to bridge the gap between the analytical and intuitive sides of their being, helping farmers to find water to nourish their crops and natural healers to know which medicines and techniques to use. Practicing divination is an ancient instinct within all humans. We all need to be able to predict our future somewhat in order to feel safe and secure.

Prepare Yourself to Ask Your Question

Calm down. Once you have decided what you want to ask, it is important that you become completely detached from any expectations you might have about what your pendulum might tell you. You have to calm yourself down to the point that all you want from your pendulum is the truth and not just the answer that you would like to hear.

Calming Technique 1

The best way to calm yourself is to close your eyes and take a few deep breaths and think the word *out* as you breathe out and then *in* as you breathe in.

Calming Technique 2

If Calming Technique 1 doesn't work for you and you find yourself very attached to your answer or you are upset for any reason, then try this ancient technique for getting in touch with your spiritual essence.

1. As you breathe slowly and calmly, realize that you are not your name; you are a soul traveling onward, and say that to yourself three times.

2. Then realize that you are not what you do for a living; you are a soul traveling onward, and say that to yourself three times.

3. Then realize that you are not what your senses are telling you every second, and say that to yourself three times.

If you carry your pendulum with you wherever you go, you will always have your magic divination tool with you when you need it. Here is how you can use it wherever and whenever you want.

Hold the cord or chain attached to the pendulum comfortably in your writing hand with your first two fingers and your thumb. Have the pendulum hang over the palm of your other hand, about two inches above it. Relax and close your eyes. In your mind, connect to the enchanted world as you imagine it. When you have put your energy into your pendulum, open your eyes.

Now focus, and ask the universe to give you your "yes" position. This will establish your personal "direction" code. It may swing clockwise or counterclockwise, going in a circular motion to indicate your "yes" answer. Alternatively, it may go from side to side or back and forth. The pendulum may exhibit different types of movement on different days or at different times of the same day.

When you have established a "yes" movement, still the pendulum by saying, "Stop," and ask for your "no" position. It will soon swing in its proper direction. Once again, your "no" answer can be different types of movement on different days or at different times of the same day.

Practice your pendulum technique by asking yes and no questions that you know the answer to. Experience will help you phrase your questions and fine-tune your accuracy.

Sometimes, when it is responding with a very strong yes or no, the pendulum will swing stronger or faster; a weaker motion will tell you that the answer is more iffy. If the answer seems iffy, phrase your question more precisely. Practice will make this easier and easier.

Remember, always try to detach from your questions and keep a clear mind, as worry can interfere with the results.

Example:

Let's say you can't find your keys. You can consult the pendulum by asking a series of questions that will reveal your answer by the process of elimination:

- Are they in the bedroom? (yes)
- Are they in the pocket of my jacket? (no)
- Are they in my handbag? (no)
- Are they next to the bed? (yes)
- Are they under something? (yes)
- Are they under the bed? (yes)

Once you have established your yes and no directions, you can ask any sort of yes or no question you can think of.

Examples of Yes and No Questions:

- Is _____ good for me?
- Did I leave my bag in the car?
- Is this vitamin good for me?
- Shall I look for a new place to live?
- Will I have a good time if I go out with Joe?
- Is my friend trustworthy?
- Is this fruit or vegetable ripe? (Suspend your pendulum over the fruit or vegetable in question.)
- Should I hire this person?
- Would I enjoy this _____? (Suspend your pendulum over the object in question.)

If possible, write down the answers you receive. If you are alone, either write them down yourself or, if you don't want to break the flow of your pendulum session, try your best to remember them.

Where Do the Answers Come From?

We believe that we all possess a truth deep within us that can perceive energy and communicate with our higher mind—it is called our intuition. The pendulum is a tool that helps to access the intuitive ability that everyone has. Every day, we all have to make inquiries about the subject of our decisions. Using a divination tool such as a pendulum can help our Higher Self communicate with the benevolent spirits around us to provide information that will enable us to know the true nature of our situation.

When you use your pendulum, you are taking part in an ancient ritual that is said to be a communication linking many levels—our conscious awareness, our subconscious, our dream selves, people and spirit guides from other times and places, and other levels of reality.

If You Have a Problem Obtaining an Answer

You may occasionally be disappointed in your ability to use your pendulum—it happens to the best dowsers. This could be due to a number of factors. Take your time and relax—the fairies don't want to be rushed, and neither should you. If you are under pressure, your tension may interfere with your pendulum results. It is very important that you remain calm, unattached to the answer you are going to get, and in a relaxed but aware mental state to attain the best results.

Also, fatigue will create false movements, so try to do your pendulum work at a time when you are not hurried, nervous, inebriated, or distracted. Practice when you are fresh and alert, not too tired, as this will also affect the outcome of your answers. Your hopes and expectations, as well as your beliefs about the world and universe, may be reflected in the pendulum movements. This is fine, as long as you are unattached to the answer that you are going to receive. If you are not, you may find yourself forcing your pendulum to go a particular way.

The pendulum can also bring up many things from your subconscious, which helps us to consider our choices and issues. However, if you are afraid of the dowsing process, perhaps because you think it is similar to the silly, made-up horror movies and television shows that have, unfortunately, become poor substitutes for fairy tales and their life lessons, then you may find yourself receiving answers that cause you to feel afraid.

If you find that the pendulum does not move well for you, be patient with yourself and your guides, and have faith. It takes most people a little while before they get the hang of it. I must confess that I was one of those people, but now it is second nature to me.

There are no rules as to exactly how and why dowsing and pendulums work, but they do, and dowsing with your pendulum is a very rewarding and positive skill to use and refine. Practice makes perfect, so practice whenever you want to make contact with the spiritual energies that guide you on your life path.

II Spirit Board Contact

Most people know what a Ouija board is. It is a trademarked rendering of the kind of "spirit board," also known as a "talking board," that has existed literally for thousands of years. Spirit boards are spiritual tools. Spirit boards have been used successfully for several thousands of years to contact the highest realms of consciousness. Until this century, their use was approached with reverence and a serious desire to acquire both knowledge and the wisdom to use it. It is said that Pythagoras (ca. 580–ca. 500 BCE), the great Greek mathematician, used a talking board of his own invention to receive some of his mathematical theorems. He and his followers believed in the survival of the soul after physical death.

Down through the centuries and in many different cultures around the world, talking boards have enjoyed immense popularity, both as amusing parlor games and as tools for serious psychic research and creativity. In the early part of the twentieth century, Patience Mather was a best-selling author whose books were known to have been written by a spirit who communicated through a talking board. More recently, the late James Merrill, author of the award-winning masterpiece of modern poetry *The Changing Light at Sandover*, openly admitted using a talking board to write it. In fact, the use of a talking board as a source of remarkable information is part of what this epic poem is about.

The late Jane Roberts, author of the priceless Seth books, as well as other writers, poets, psychic researchers, and literally millions of people, have used talking boards to help them open up to new possibilities about the survival of the soul and psyche. We created our series of talking boards to remedy deficiencies in the talking board sets previously in use. One of the most glaring deficiencies is the absence of proper instructions, something we have gone to great pains to remedy on these pages.

You can use one of the three talking boards that we have invented—*The Psychic Circle*, *The Pathfinder Psychic Talking Board*, or *The Enchanted Spellboard*—or you can make one yourself.

To Make Your Own Spirit Board

You will need a large piece of paper, approximately fifteen by twenty inches, and a large piece of glass or Plexiglas cut to the same size. Make sure to have all the points and edges polished smooth to avoid cutting yourself. You will also need a black Magic Marker and a small drinking glass, turned upside down, to use for the indicator.

Simply write out the alphabet and numbers one to nine along with the words *yes, no,* and *good-bye* on the paper, and cover it with the Plexiglas. Place the inverted drinking glass on top.

1. Position the spirit board so that anyone using it will be able to move the glass planchette, or indicator, around the entire board comfortably.

2. Make sure that your board and indicator glass are clean and free of dust or dirt.

3. Before you begin your session, prepare the main questions you intend to ask. Have some way of recording the answers, too. The information you receive will depend on how clearly and simply you phrase your questions. Plan on starting your session with questions that can be answered with either "yes" or "no."

4. Always say a prayer or perform some other ritual prior to your session to dispel any negative energy in or around you.

5. If you are using the spirit board by yourself, then place both of your index fingers gently on the upside-down drinking glass, planchette, or indicator. If two people are working the spirit board, they should each use the index finger of one hand. Do not press hard—a light touch works best.

6. Start your session by asking your yes or no question. You can then ask for a message from spirit. After you've asked your question, stay calm, as you will soon feel the glass move as if by itself, hovering over the letters to spell out words in answer to your question. If you get too excited or are not sure of the meaning of your answer, ask yes or no questions to calm yourself and to act as confirmation.

7. You must always properly close your session with the spirit board. Rather than just removing your hands from the planchette, say out loud or to yourself, "Blessed be," or "Good-bye and thank you."

Chinese Zodiac

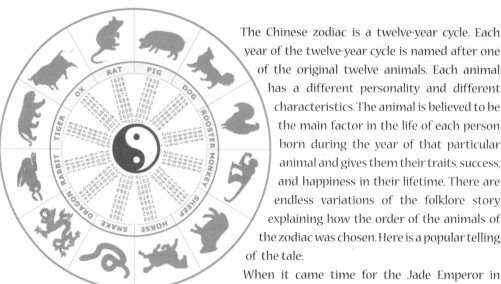

The Chinese zodiac is a twelve-year cycle. Each year of the twelve-year cycle is named after one of the original twelve animals. Each animal has a different personality and different characteristics. The animal is believed to be the main factor in the life of each person born during the year of that particular animal and gives them their traits, success, and happiness in their lifetime. There are endless variations of the folklore story explaining how the order of the animals of the zodiac was chosen. Here is a popular telling of the tale:

When it came time for the Jade Emperor in Heaven to decide the order of the zodiac, he invited all the animals to participate in a race. The order of the zodiac would be decided by the order in which animals finished the race.

When the competition started, the ox was leading the pack, but the rat jumped on his back. Since the rat was so light and small, the ox did not realize that the rat was hitching a ride. As the ox approached the finish line, the rat leapt off his back and was crowned as the first animal to complete the race.

After all the creatures finished the race, the order was finalized: rat, ox, tiger, rabbit, dragon, snake, horse, goat, monkey, rooster, dog, and pig.

According to legend, those born in a particular year of an animal are said to possess particular character traits associated with that animal. Check the Chinese zodiac calendar (see pages 81–85) to see what your sign is.

1. RAT

Forthright, disciplined, systematic, meticulous, charismatic, hardworking, industrious, charming, eloquent, sociable, shrewd. Can be manipulative, vindictive, mendacious, venal, selfish, obstinate, critical, overambitious, ruthless, intolerant, scheming.

People born in the Year of the Rat are noted for their charm and attraction for the opposite sex. They work hard to achieve their goals and acquire possessions, and they are likely to be perfectionists. They are basically thrifty with money. Rat people are easily angered and love to gossip. Their ambitions are big, and they are usually very successful.

2. OX

Dependable, calm, methodical, patient, hardworking, ambitious, conventional, steady, modest, logical, resolute, tenacious. Can be stubborn, narrow-minded, materialistic, rigid, demanding.

People born in the Year of the Ox are patient and inspire confidence in others. They tend, however, to be eccentric and bigoted, and they anger easily. They have fierce tempers, and although they speak little, when they do they are quite eloquent. Ox people are mentally and physically alert. Generally easygoing, they can be remarkably stubborn, and they hate to fail or be opposed.

3. TIGER

Unpredictable, rebellious, colorful, powerful, passionate, daring, impulsive, vigorous, stimulating, sincere, affectionate, humanitarian, generous. Can be restless, reckless, impatient, quick-tempered, obstinate, and selfish.

Tiger people are sensitive, given to deep thinking, capable of great sympathy. They can be extremely short-tempered, however. Other people have great respect for them, but sometimes tiger people come into conflict with older people or those in authority. Sometimes people born in the Year of the Tiger cannot make up their minds, which can result in a poor, hasty decision or a sound decision arrived at too late. They are suspicious of others, but they are courageous and powerful.

4. RABBIT

Gracious, kind, sensitive, soft-spoken, amiable, elegant, reserved, cautious, artistic, thorough, tender, self-assured, astute, compassionate, flexible. Can be moody, detached, superficial, self-indulgent, opportunistic, and lazy.

People born in the Year of the Rabbit are articulate, talented, and ambitious. They are virtuous and reserved and have excellent taste. Rabbit people are admired and trusted and are often financially lucky. They are fond of gossip but are tactful and generally kind. Rabbit people seldom lose their temper. They are clever at business and, being conscientious, never back out of a contract. They would make good gamblers, for they have the uncanny gift of choosing the right thing. However, they seldom gamble, as they are conservative and wise.

5. DRAGON

Magnanimous, stately, vigorous, strong, self-assured, proud, noble, direct, dignified, zealous, fiery, passionate, decisive, pioneering, ambitious, generous, loyal. Can be arrogant, imperious, tyrannical, demanding, eccentric, grandiloquent and extremely bombastic, prejudiced, dogmatic, overbearing, violent, impetuous, brash.

People born in the Year of the Dragon are healthy, energetic, excitable, short-tempered, and stubborn. They are also honest, sensitive, and brave, and they inspire confidence and trust. Dragon people are the most eccentric of any in the Eastern zodiac. They neither borrow money nor make flowery speeches, but they tend to be softhearted, which sometimes gives others an advantage over them.

6. SNAKE

Deep thinking, wise, mystical, graceful, soft-spoken, sensual, creative, prudent, shrewd, ambitious, elegant, cautious, responsible, calm, strong, constant, purposeful. Can be a loner, bad communicator, possessive, hedonistic, self-doubting, distrustful, mendacious.

People born in the Year of the Snake are deep. They say little and possess great wisdom. Snake people are often quite vain, selfish, and a bit stingy. Yet they have tremendous sympathy for others and try to help those less fortunate. Snake people tend to overdo, since they have doubts about other people's judgment and prefer to rely on themselves. They are determined in whatever they do and hate to fail. Though calm on the surface, they are intense and passionate.

7. HORSE

 Cheerful, popular, quick-witted, changeable, earthy, perceptive, talkative, mentally and physically agile, magnetic, intelligent, astute, flexible, open-minded. Can be fickle, arrogant, anxious, rude, gullible, stubborn.

People born in the Year of the Horse are popular. They are cheerful, skillful with money, and perceptive, although they sometimes talk too much. They are wise, talented, and good with their hands, and sometimes have a weakness for members of the opposite sex. They are impatient and hot-blooded about everything except their daily work. They like entertainment and large crowds. They are very independent and rarely listen to advice.

8. GOAT

 Righteous, sincere, sympathetic, mild-mannered, shy, artistic, creative, gentle, compassionate, understanding, mothering, determined, peaceful, generous, seekers of security. Can be moody, indecisive, overpassive, worrier, pessimistic, oversensitive, complainer, wise.

People born in the Year of the Goat are elegant and highly accomplished in the arts. Goat people are often shy, pessimistic, and puzzled about life. They are usually deeply spiritual, yet timid by nature. Sometimes clumsy in speech, they are always passionate about what they do and what they believe in. Goat people never have to worry about having the best in life, for their abilities make money for them, and they are able to enjoy the creature comforts that they like.

9. MONKEY

 Inventor, motivator, improviser, quick-witted, inquisitive, flexible, innovative, problem solver, self-assured, sociable, polite, dignified, competitive, objective, factual, intellectual. Can be egotistical, vain, selfish, reckless, snobbish, deceptive, manipulative, cunning, jealous, and suspicious.

People born in the Year of the Monkey are clever, skillful, and flexible. They are remarkably inventive and original and can solve the most difficult problems with ease. They want to do things now, and if they cannot get started immediately, they become discouraged and sometimes leave their projects. Having common sense, Monkey people have a deep desire for knowledge and have excellent memories.

10. ROOSTER

Acute, neat, meticulous, organized, self-assured, decisive, conservative, critical, perfectionist, alert, zealous, practical, scientific, responsible. Can be overzealous and critical, puritanical, egotistical, abrasive, opinionated.

People born in the Year of the Rooster are deep thinkers, capable, and talented. They like to be busy and are devoted beyond their capabilities and are deeply disappointed if they fail. They frequently are loners and are often a bit eccentric. They can be selfish and too outspoken but are always interesting and can be extremely brave.

11. DOG

Honest, intelligent, straight-forward, loyal, sense of justice and fair play, attractive, amicable, unpretentious, sociable, open-minded, idealistic, moralistic, practical, affectionate, dogged. Can be cynical, lazy, cold, judgmental, pessimistic, worrier, stubborn, and quarrelsome.

People born in the Year of the Dog possess the best traits of human nature. They have a deep sense of loyalty, are honest, and inspire confidence because they know how to keep secrets. But Dog people are also somewhat selfish, terribly stubborn, and eccentric. They can be cold emotionally and sometimes distant at parties.

They can find fault with many things and are noted for their sharp tongues. Dog people make good leaders.

12. PIG

Honest, simple, gallant, sturdy, sociable, peace-loving, patient, loyal, hard-working, trusting, sincere, calm, understanding, thoughtful, scrupulous, passionate, intelligent. Can be naive, overreliant, self-indulgent, gullible, fatalistic, and materialistic.

People born in the Year of the Pig are chivalrous and gallant. Whatever they do, they do with all their strength and with great honesty. They don't make many friends, but they make them for life, and anyone having a Pig Year friend is fortunate, for they are extremely loyal. They don't talk much but have a great thirst for knowledge and are generally well-informed. Pig people are quick-tempered, yet they hate arguments and quarreling. They are kind to their loved ones.

Chinese Zodiac Calendar

YEAR	SIGN	ELEMENT	YEAR BEGINS	YEAR ENDS
1901	Ox	Metal	2/19/1901	2/7/1902
1902	Tiger	Water	2/8/1902	1/28/1903
1903	Cat	Water	1/29/1903	2/15/1904
1904	Dragon	Wood	2/16/1904	2/3/1905
1905	Snake	Wood	2/4/1905	1/24/1906
1906	Horse	Fire	1/25/1906	2/12/1907
1907	Goat	Fire	2/13/1907	2/1/1908
1908	Monkey	Earth	2/2/1908	1/21/1909
1909	Rooster	Earth	1/22/1909	2/9/1910
1910	Dog	Metal	2/10/1910	1/29/1911
1911	Pig	Metal	1/30/1911	2/17/1912
1912	Rat	Water	2/18/1912	2/5/1913
1913	Ox	Water	2/6/1913	1/25/1914
1914	Tiger	Wood	1/26/1914	2/13/1915
1915	Cat	Wood	2/14/1915	2/2/1916
1916	Dragon	Fire	2/3/1916	1/22/1917
1917	Snake	Fire	1/23/1917	2/10/1918
1918	Horse	Earth	2/11/1918	1/31/1919
1919	Goat	Earth	2/1/1919	2/19/1920
1920	Monkey	Metal	2/20/1920	2/7/1921
1921	Rooster	Metal	2/8/1921	1/27/1922
1922	Dog	Water	1/28/1922	2/15/1923
1923	Pig	Water	2/16/1923	2/4/1924
1924	Rat	Wood	2/5/1924	1/23/1925
1925	Ox	Wood	1/24/1925	2/12/1926
1926	Tiger	Fire	2/13/1926	2/1/1927
1927	Cat	Fire	2/2/1927	1/22/1928
1928	Dragon	Earth	1/23/1928	2/9/1929

Chinese Zodiac

YEAR	SIGN	ELEMENT	YEAR BEGINS	YEAR ENDS
1929	Snake	Earth	2/10/1929	1/29/1930
1930	Horse	Metal	1/30/1930	2/16/1931
1931	Goat	Metal	2/17/1931	2/5/1932
1932	Monkey	Water	2/6/1932	1/25/1933
1933	Rooster	Water	1/26/1933	2/13/1934
1934	Dog	Wood	2/14/1934	2/3/1935
1935	Pig	Wood	2/4/1935	1/23/1936
1936	Rat	Fire	1/24/1936	2/10/1937
1937	Ox	Fire	2/11/1937	1/30/1938
1938	Tiger	Earth	1/31/1938	2/18/1939
1939	Cat	Earth	2/19/1939	2/7/1940
1940	Dragon	Metal	2/8/1940	1/26/1941
1941	Snake	Metal	1/27/1941	2/14/1942
1942	Horse	Water	2/15/1942	2/4/1943
1943	Goat	Water	2/5/1943	1/24/1944
1944	Monkey	Wood	1/25/1944	2/12/1945
1945	Rooster	Wood	2/13/1945	2/1/1946
1946	Dog	Fire	2/2/1946	1/21/1947
1947	Pig	Fire	1/22/1947	2/9/1948
1948	Rat	Earth	2/10/1948	1/28/1949
1949	Ox	Earth	1/29/1949	2/16/1950
1950	Tiger	Metal	2/17/1950	2/5/1951
1951	Cat	Metal	2/6/1951	1/26/1952
1952	Dragon	Water	1/27/1952	2/13/1953
1953	Snake	Water	2/14/1953	2/2/1954
1954	Horse	Wood	2/3/1954	1/23/1955
1955	Goat	Wood	1/24/1955	2/11/1956
1956	Monkey	Fire	2/12/1956	1/30/1957
1957	Rooster	Fire	1/31/1957	2/17/1958
1958	Dog	Earth	2/18/1958	2/7/1959

33 Ways to Tell Your Future

YEAR	SIGN	ELEMENT	YEAR BEGINS	YEAR ENDS
1959	Pig	Earth	2/8/1959	1/27/1960
1960	Rat	Metal	1/28/1960	2/14/1961
1961	Ox	Metal	2/15/1961	2/4/1962
1962	Tiger	Water	2/5/1962	1/24/1963
1963	Cat	Water	1/25/1963	2/12/1964
1964	Dragon	Wood	2/13/1964	2/1/1965
1965	Snake	Wood	2/2/1965	1/20/1966
1966	Horse	Fire	1/21/1966	2/8/1967
1967	Goat	Fire	2/9/1967	1/29/1968
1968	Monkey	Earth	1/30/1968	2/16/1969
1969	Rooster	Earth	2/17/1969	2/5/1970
1970	Dog	Metal	2/6/1970	1/26/1971
1971	Pig	Metal	1/27/1971	2/14/1972
1972	Rat	Water	2/15/1972	2/2/1973
1973	Ox	Water	2/3/1973	1/22/1974
1974	Tiger	Wood	1/23/1974	2/10/1975
1975	Cat	Wood	2/11/1975	1/30/1976
1976	Dragon	Fire	1/31/1976	2/17/1977
1977	Snake	Fire	2/18/1977	2/6/1978
1978	Horse	Earth	2/7/1978	1/27/1979
1979	Goat	Earth	1/28/1979	2/15/1980
1980	Monkey	Metal	2/16/1980	2/4/1981
1981	Rooster	Metal	2/5/1981	1/24/1982
1982	Dog	Water	1/25/1982	2/12/1983
1983	Pig	Water	2/13/1983	2/1/1984
1984	Rat	Wood	2/2/1984	2/19/1985
1985	Ox	Wood	2/20/1985	2/8/1986
1986	Tiger	Fire	2/9/1986	1/28/1987
1987	Cat	Fire	1/29/1987	2/16/1988
1988	Dragon	Earth	2/17/1988	2/5/1989

YEAR	SIGN	ELEMENT	YEAR BEGINS	YEAR ENDS
1989	Snake	Earth	2/6/1989	1/26/1990
1990	Horse	Metal	1/27/1990	2/14/1991
1991	Goat	Metal	2/15/1991	2/3/1992
1992	Monkey	Water	2/4/1992	1/22/1993
1993	Rooster	Water	1/23/1993	2/9/1994
1994	Dog	Wood	2/10/1994	1/30/1995
1995	Pig	Wood	1/31/1995	2/18/1996
1996	Rat	Fire	2/19/1996	2/6/1997
1997	Ox	Fire	2/7/1997	1/27/1998
1998	Tiger	Earth	1/28/1998	2/15/1999
1999	Cat	Earth	2/16/1999	2/4/2000
2000	Dragon	Metal	2/5/2000	1/23/2001
2001	Snake	Metal	1/24/2001	2/11/2002
2002	Horse	Water	2/12/2002	1/31/2003
2003	Goat	Water	2/1/2003	1/21/2004
2004	Monkey	Wood	1/22/2004	2/8/2005
2005	Rooster	Wood	2/9/2005	1/28/2006
2006	Dog	Fire	1/29/2006	2/17/2007
2007	Pig	Fire	2/18/2007	2/6/2008
2008	Rat	Earth	2/7/2008	1/25/2009
2009	Ox	Earth	1/26/2009	2/13/2010
2010	Tiger	Metal	2/14/2010	2/2/2011
2011	Cat	Metal	2/3/2011	1/22/2012
2012	Dragon	Water	1/23/2012	2/9/2013
2013	Snake	Water	2/10/2013	1/30/2014
2014	Horse	Wood	1/31/2014	2/18/2015
2015	Goat	Wood	2/19/2015	2/7/2016
2016	Monkey	Fire	2/8/2016	1/27/2017
2017	Rooster	Fire	1/28/2017	2/15/2018
2018	Dog	Earth	2/16/2018	2/4/2019
2019	Pig	Earth	2/5/2019	1/24/2020

33 *Ways to Tell Your Future*

Number Symbolism

13

Numbers are both magical and practical. We use them to keep track of sensible things and to count our blessings, dreams, and wishes. Numbers keep us grounded, and they have sent us to the Moon. No matter in what way we use them, we can't do without them. By their very nature, numbers can bring us in touch with the magical, enchanted world we all inhabit. They have a powerful symbolic meaning, and when a number appears systematically over and over again, attention should be paid to it. If a number seems to recur in your life, please read it's meaning below. Because each of these numbers, from zero to nine, has its own significance, you can use them to get closer to nature, to your spiritual guides, and to a more magical life.

0

Zero, by itself, equals nothing, of course, and yet it encompasses the promise of everything. Even though zero is not technically a number, it is the number of the absolute. It is a powerful force for order. It symbolizes the principle of profound transformation and spiritual change. It represents both the unplanned and the unknowable. This symbol has no beginning and no end, so it signifies the reality beyond time, as well as being in the moment. It is the symbol of dichotomy, the ellipse of its two sides signifying both rise and fall, evolution and devolution. It stands for both a lack of substance and boundless, unlimited potential. Zero can suggest either great knowledge or a lack of knowledge. When it presents itself in a seemingly coincidental manner, pay attention to what you may think is only "nothing."

1

The number one is the number of self, of initiation and beginnings. It represents the individual, singular hopes and dreams, strength of will, and deliberate separateness. This is a time to stand alone, to stand up for personal beliefs and goals. One represents the need to focus on talents and abilities without being afraid of being singled out. It suggests strong ambition, the will to achieve, and a great appetite for success. One emphasizes individuality, as in "one of a kind." This number can also signify a time of singular purpose. Self-interest is suggested, although this does not have to translate to selfishness. Its energy is unique, undeterred, and idiosyncratic.

2

The number two is a symbol of duality, partnership, and harmony, as well as polarity. It can signify two people coming together in a relationship, or two people working apart as opposites. It is indicative of strength through redoubled effort. The number two signifies a time in life when the individual is ready to embrace emotional intimacy. It symbolizes a willingness and ability to become aware of the needs of others. Cooperation, diplomacy, service, support, and teamwork as a couple are all emphasized, as are the principles of feminine-masculine dichotomy known by the Chinese as yin and yang. Its energy is shared, materialistic, grounded, and practical but may also be overprotective, jealous, and codependent.

3

The number three indicates energy being channeled in a way that is active and fluent and will lead toward a swift conclusion. This number is highly positive, charming, energetic, and fun loving. It represents communication and information on every level— from gossip to enlightenment. It is sometimes referred to as the "heavenly" number because it is symbolic of the Holy Trinity in the Christian tradition. The number three also signifies the melding of mind-body-spirit energy. Because it is formed by the combination of the number one, signifying independence, and the number two, which evokes strength through togetherness, three represents the principles of growth, fruitfulness, creativity, and longevity. It also signifies the triangle, the strongest structure, and completion. Its energy is mutable, fast moving, and eclectic.

4

The number four is a stable number that represents the underpinnings of things that are logical, systematic, and orderly. Because patience, responsibility, and even serenity are indicated, it can help in a time of limitations and difficulty. Since four is made up of two plus two, it represents work and productivity as well as all the accomplishments that come from these efforts. The number represents the shape of the square, each angle in perfect harmony with the others. It suggests the accord of people working together in group conditions, as well as the support that is required and expected when people are dependent on one another. The energy of the number four is cohesive, orderly, and balanced, though sometimes stagnant.

5

The number five symbolizes adventure, creative energy, passion, and an optimistic point of view. It represents constantly shifting activity as well as nontraditional behavior and unconventional ideas. The number five has a certain esoteric quality as well, since it signifies the pentagram, a five-sided star often used in rituals and spell making. It also calls to mind the five senses. The number is representative of attachments, sexual assignations, physical attraction, and romantic perfection. Five can symbolize a talented, artistic individual who may also be self-indulgent, undependable, and morally weak. Alternatively, it can suggest a genius or a person of many special gifts. The energy of five is spontaneous, undisciplined, changeable, and liberating.

6

The number six is a harmonious number that suggests equilibrium and security. Because it is a duality of the number three, it is symbolic of tradition, stability, and support. It also represents familial love, marriage, family responsibilities, and happiness, which are based on security.

Six can also suggest a period in life where there is a return to familiar surroundings or typically conventional behavior and attitudes after a time of separation or rebellion. Because it is known as "humankind's number," it symbolizes struggles or achievements on a material level. The number six is also reflective of an individual who is a teacher, or someone who acts in the capacity of a mentor or adviser. Its energy is health giving, conservative, and deliberate.

7

The number seven is generally regarded as a spiritual number because of its frequent mention in the Bible. It also reflects tranquility, self-expression, and a philosophical point of view. It can symbolize a period of germination when one's thinking has evolved to the spiritual level. Seven is the number of inventors, scientists, thinkers, and eccentrics. It is associated with truth seeking and contemplation and can symbolize a time of being alone, but in the way of preparing for initiation into a new situation or

a debut. The number reflects the spiritual and the material world as well as the transition between the two. Its energy is dreamy and psychic, and care must be taken to avoid dubious or deceptive situations.

8

The number eight is reflective of power, abundance, and success as well as the principle of domination and control. Because its shape forms the sign for infinity, it also has esoteric significance. It represents questions and their answers as well as the secrets that are contained in both. Eight symbolizes material matters as well as that which is strictly theoretical. The number can represent an individual who has strong leadership and executive skills, a decision maker who relies as much on intuition as on facts. It can symbolize a legacy, either material or magical in form. The power of eight is in its ability to transcend the boundaries of the practical world while still representing it. Its energy is formal and intractable.

9

The number nine is representative of the principles of healing, artistry, and knowledge. It can symbolize the philosopher or the physician, someone whose mission it is to cure all the ills of the world. This may also signify a selfless and romantic individual who is a dreamer and a doer, a person with the proverbial heart of gold. It can indicate a time of idealism when both inspiration and intuition serve as tools for altruistic purposes. Nine is the number of metaphysics and also represents the dabbler and the dilettante, whose methods may be unconventional or inexperienced, yet wholehearted. The energy of nine is compassionate and global but can also be naive and unstable.

Numerology: Name

14

Every name given to a human being has a correspondence in numbers. Probably the person who started that catchy slang phrase "I've got your number" had not the remotest idea that it contained a profound occult truth. There is a psychological reason behind everything, if we only knew it.

Each letter of a name has its own numerical value, and the method given here of working out the value of names is simple—it's the same one that has been used by students of the Kabbalah and wisdom teachers from time immemorial. The results of their tests, which have been handed down to us, have been found so accurate that even skeptics and scoffers can but listen respectfully to deductions made by these wise men of old.

The following is a table of the values of the letters of the English alphabet as it stands today, corresponding to the values of the same letters in great part as they were in other languages of antiquity when numerology was first formulated:

A	B	C	D	E	F	G	H	I	J	K	L	M	N	O	P	Q	R	S	T	U	V	W	X	Y	Z
1	2	2	4	5	8	3	8	1	1	2	3	4	5	7	8	1	2	3	4	6	6	6	6	1	7

Each name must be written vertically, and if an individual has three or more names, a separate column is made for each name. Against each letter is placed its corresponding number. Then, beginning with the last letter of each name and going upward, assigning the last letter the number 1, the second-to-last letter the number 2, the third-to-last letter the number 3, and so on, the numbers assigned to each letter are multiplied.

For example:

$$\begin{aligned}
\textbf{M} \quad 4 \times 4 &= 16 \\
\textbf{A} \quad 1 \times 3 &= 3 \\
\textbf{R} \quad 2 \times 2 &= 4 \\
\textbf{Y} \quad 1 \times 1 &= 1 \\
\hline
24 \quad &2 + 4 = 6
\end{aligned}$$

You can see that in the name Mary the number 24 becomes 6 when the two digits are added together.

By the simple system fully explained here, you can calculate the value of your own name (and that of anyone in whom you are interested), and judge just how far it will be to your happiness and advantage to pursue a relationship with them, whether in friendship, marriage, or business.

A person with a name—either a given or family name—in which the letter *A* is the first letter, or occurs often in the name, will be a dominant and striking personality, full of courage and love of adventure, and creative in some line of endeavor, but will have a certain hardness and harshness. This person will have great endurance, power of resistance, and intense feelings.

The *E* often repeated, or the *E* as the first letter, gives a highly nervous temperament, fertile imagination, love of art and beauty, restless, not always easy to get along with, not physically strong, very responsive to outer conditions, highly impressionable, sometimes psychic, and excitable.

When the letter *I* is most in evidence, there is an unfailing sense of humor and a keen wit, often sarcastic. The person has a scientific, analytical mind, intuition, quick perception, a literary trend, and delight in argument, and can be critical.

The letter *O* is the sign of universal brotherhood, the truly charitable mind, the soul of the world, calmness, depth, and breadth. It is the sign of a soul that has learned its lessons through many rebirths.

The letter *U* has something of the same significance as *O*, as it is very similar in sound vibration, but is not of as great potency. It also has something of the vibration of *E*.

In marriage, an ideal blending is the *A* and *E* in the names of both the man and woman, for these are the two poles, masculine and feminine. There should also be the *I* and *O* for intellect and soul development.

Where the letter *A* predominates in the names of both the husband and wife, there will be a struggle for supremacy. If there are too many *E*'s, there will be a great deal of unnecessary friction, and if there are too many *I*'s, the sharpness of intellect will be like the striking together of flint—sparks but no warmth. If there are many *O*'s, they will unite in some humanitarian work and will love their neighbors as themselves.

Numerology: Birth Date

15

In the same way that we set up a chart that enables us to make a person's name indicate that person's character, so can we set up a birth chart to give additional information concerning character and ability. To do this, we should know the person's year, month, and date of birth, because the year alone, or the day alone, will disclose only vague facts.

Suppose that you wish to set up a chart for an individual who was born March 13, 1952. The months are numbered 1 to 12; the days are numbered 1 to 31; the years are designated according to their appearance upon the Gregorian calendar. Hence, you set up the chart as follows:

March	13	1952
3	4	8

$$3 + 4 + 8 = 15 = 6$$

If your birth chart vibrates to the same number as your name chart, you may be sure that this number is a strong indication of character. If your birth chart comes under another digit from your name chart, there will be a fairly close following of the digit of your birth chart, yet not such a strong following as when both numbers are the same.

Numbers 1 to 9

1

One is the number of POWER, individuality, harmony, activity, and construction. The person whose name vibrates to this number is distinctive and highly individualized, a thinker, a creator, no matter in what sphere he or she may be placed. In those who do not come up to the highest vibrations of this powerful number, it manifests itself in egotism, too much self-consciousness, arrogance, and dominance. Its element is fire.

Keywords
Willingness, courage, conviction, self-control, leadership, challenges, conquering, self-esteem, success, control

2

Two is the number of COMMUNICATION, intellect, perception of truth, awakening of consciousness, the dual principle of life, the union of male and female, emotion, attraction, and repulsion. It is the number of marriage. Two is a peacemaker and people whose name vibrates to this number will at times go out of their way to ensure that everything around them is running smoothly. Two gives empathy for the feelings of others and will be considerate of others. Its element is air.

Keywords
Empathy, home, harmony, peace, congenial, humanitarian, protector, safety, communications, ability, partnership

3

Three is the number of WISDOM. It signifies love in its highest and purest form, tenderness, sympathy, harmony, fruitfulness and plenty, riches, and success. It is a beautiful and fortunate number. There is also an intellectual side to the nature of three, that thirst to find the answers to the questions in life. People whose name vibrates to the number three are also good negotiators. Its element is water.

Keywords
Interesting, knowledge, intelligence, guidance, determination, negotiator, successful, dissatisfaction, authority, clear-sighted

4

Four is the number of COMPLETION, realization of ambitions, things accomplished, stability, security, protection, materiality, and acquisition of property and possessions. Those who come under this vibration are strong, firm of purpose, honorable, inflexible, just, and sincere. Four can build things up or can tear things down, if they are not up to four's standard. Its element is earth.

Keywords
Builder, humanitarian, destruction, perfectionist, sincerity, happiness, leadership, quality, functional, gentle, caring

5

Five is an intense vibration, a magical number of CHANGE. Those whose names respond to the vibrations of five must, above all things, learn self-control, self-mastery, calmness, and moderation, and must turn the dynamic force of this number into the right channels or it may upset the nervous system. When working under the direction of true wisdom, five is a tremendous force for good, for healing, and for the guidance of others. The element is fire.

Keywords

Conviction, constant, renewal, spiritually aware, destiny, choice, self-discovery, crossroads, organization, achievement

6

Six is the number of COMPASSION. It is a beautiful vibration, giving appreciation of all that is beautiful and artistic, and happiness in love and marriage. People whose names respond to this vibration are good when times are tough, as they can see the truth in any given situation, and know exactly what to do when called upon to act in times of crisis. Nature may also be important to a six, for you care for your environment and don't wish it to be destroyed. The element is air.

Keywords

Honesty, tough, hardworking, nurturing, love, nature, pollution, solutions, development, humanity, compassion

7

Seven is the number of RECOGNITION and has been held as a sacred number in every religion and all wisdom teachings. People whose names respond to the vibration of the number seven have gathered a wealth of experience and know how to put those experiences into practice. Not only is seven the number of earthly splendor and royalty, but it is the highest number of wisdom, understanding, and perfection. The element of the number seven is fire.

Keywords

Philosophy, routine, practice, consume, search, acquiring, answers, mystical, reclusive, physical, gratification

8

Eight is the number of COURAGE. In its highest form it is the expression of inspiration, invention, and genius. Those whose names have the value of eight nearly always do very important work in the world. They are living centers of power, but not by any means of peace. No matter what happens, they are able to pick up the pieces and start again. The element of this number is air.

Keywords

Perseverance, courage, rewards, ambition, problem solver, good times, happiness, smiling, gentleness, encouragement

9

Nine is the number of PEACE and regeneration; it represents the psychic plane, mysticism, clairvoyance, clairaudience, intuition, the sixth sense, dreams, telepathy, and predictions. When the wisdom and philosophy are turned to the enlightenment of others, it is a great power, but unless rightly directed there is apt to be obsession. Those whose name number is nine should study, teach, and write. The element of nine is water.

Keywords

Humanity, inner knowledge, depth, inspiring, peace, harmony, goodness, worthy, universal love, faith, contentment

16

Graphology: Handwriting Analysis

One of the proven methods of analyzing character is from a person's handwriting. This science, called graphology, is devoted to the judging of a person's character, disposition, and aptitude from specimens of his or her handwriting. Graphology is an invaluable aid in business, and a source of great gratification in private and social life.

As general guides, the following rules should be observed. An ideal specimen of a person's handwriting should be written in black or very dark ink, with the favorite pen of the writer, on white, unruled paper. It should be a natural piece of writing and not one written especially for display as penmanship. It is preferable to have several pages of writing, although a reading can be made even from a signature.

For a complete analysis, it is wise to have a sample of the person's writing that spans a period of years, as this makes it possible to trace changes in character and to affirm suppositions. Writing on an envelope is rarely a satisfactory sample, as envelopes are generally addressed with more than ordinary care. Also, when writing covers a series of pages, the writing on the last page is usually the most natural, as most people begin a letter with careful, meticulous characters and then lapse into their normal handwriting.

What Your Handwriting Shows

Size

The relation between writing and character is often quite direct. People who consider details rather than large classifications have small handwriting, forming low letters. When the writing is very small, it denotes an unusual power of concentration. Authors generally write small hands, showing a grasp of minute details in depicting the lives of their characters.

High letters indicate a mind for generalizations. In any writing, when a person makes each letter the same size, it denotes a conscientious person. When writing shows a tendency to grow gradually smaller, or larger, it indicates finesse. When words taper so much that they become illegible, they show a crafty mind. The writing of a lazy person also tapers, except that the words end in mere lines as the person avoids the effort of creating individual letters.

Tact is indicated when the first letter of every word is larger than the others. When upper-loop letters, such as *l*, *h*, and *k*, are written high above the small letters, it denotes a keen imagination. When these letters are low, not mounting to twice the average size of the small letters, it indicates a lack of imagination, and a person of practical, prosaic tendencies. The lengths of the lower-loop letters, such as *g*, *q*, and *y*, reflect the physical activity of the writer. If they are short, they show a tendency to sluggishness and too little exercise. When long, they indicate a love of manual exertion and bodily activity.

Slope

The slope of writing, which means the angle of its deviation from the exact vertical, or the angle of its slant, reflects the secrets of the heart. A slope to the right indicates the presence of an affectionate nature. This is practically a universal tendency and can be seen in the handwriting of nearly all people. Should the writing slope decidedly to the right, it denotes a rich emotional nature with affections easily touched.

When the writing is straight up and down, that is, quite vertical, it shows a cold nature, one indifferent to affection. The exceptions to this rule are those cases where children were taught to write that way. However, even these soon lapse into their natural handwriting, as soon as they go out into the world.

The less the slope, the more frigid the nature, so that a natural backhand style of writing shows a lack of emotions. This, however, is not a hard-and-fast rule and should be considered in connection with other factors, such as someone who writes left-handed. Sometimes a shock to the emotions, such as a frustrated love affair, or the death of a beloved one, will swing a handwriting to this direction temporarily.

When the strokes in the small and large letters maintain the same slant, it denotes a consistent character. When the small letters point in one direction, and the slope of the large ones in another, it shows a variable and moody character.

Lines

By line, we mean the imaginary line at the base of any specimen of writing upon which the letters are supposed to rest. That is why ruled paper should not be used, as any person will hug the drawn line in writing and thus eliminate an important clue to analysis.

The ability to maintain a straight line in writing on unruled paper indicates a person with an honest, direct nature. When the line of writing is irregular, it denotes not necessarily a dishonest person, but one who is guarded and secretive and prefers a roundabout way of getting at things.

Ascending writing that mounts up the page shows a buoyant spirit, probably in the cradle of some high hopes for wealth and honor. When the lines are fairly horizontal but the words end in a droop, it denotes a spirit in a mood of despair or dejection. This is not a permanent trait, but usually the result of some temporary misfortune. This droop is most commonly found in the writing of women, inasmuch as they are so much more susceptible to the winds and hazards of romance than men.

If the writing descends a great deal, it shows a despondent and melancholy nature. Where the words descend more than the lines, it depicts a struggle between a naturally optimistic nature and a period of depression. When the lines descend more than the words, it shows a weary nature, one sated with life and its pleasures.

Shape

Shape refers to group rather than individual letters. Writing that is compressed, in which the vertical strokes are close together, shows a nature that is reserved and keeps largely to itself. Such people do not encourage ready friendships and do not invite advice. When the strokes are generously spaced, so that the letters are wider than they are long, it is an indication of an open, hospitable nature.

A squareness in letters shows a precise mind, one that can easily absorb scientific facts. Such people also make good mechanics and are at home among machines and mechanical devices.

When small letters are pointed at the top, the writer is alert to all his or her surroundings, and naturally perceives things keenly. When they are rounded at the top, the subject is rather blunt and dulled. When letters are pointed at the bottom, it shows a curious nature. When they are rounded at the bottom, this quality is absent. When round letters are accompanied by an even swing of the pen, it signifies a sense of rhythm and a fondness for music.

When such letters as *o*, *a*, and *d* are closed at the top, the writer has a secretive nature and rarely opens his or her lips. When these letters are open at the top, the subject speaks readily of his or her own affairs. Letters open at the bottom have been known to show a hypocritical nature, one not to be trusted.

33 Ways to Tell Your Future

A long beginning stroke before each word shows a hurried, impatient nature. Where these beginnings are omitted entirely, the nature is that of a slow, deliberate person.

When the cross strokes—the bar used to cross the small letter *t* and the capitals *A* and *H*—are made very dark and definite, they denote a strong, dominant personality. People who omit them are generally very humble and are content to do humdrum tasks. When the cross stroke is straight and even on both sides of the *t*, it denotes a thoughtful and methodical nature. A lighter, airier nature will make fancy twists to the cross stroke. When the final strokes are long, the subject is fond of humor.

The stroke, which is normally horizontal, is sometimes drawn at an angle. When it ascends, it denotes ambition and pride. When the ascent is so steep as to point upward, it denotes an ability to imitate others. When the bar descends, it shows a drooping nature, one not impelled to progress. One that points definitely downward shows a self-satisfied, opinionated person.

A small hook at the end of words shows a tenacious nature. People who let their imaginations run away with them and are prone to boasting and exaggerating show it in their writing by large loops and strokes. When letters are gone over for repairs, such as correcting a letter here and there, which may look sloppy, the writer is a person eager to improve himself.

Spacing

Spacing may be either horizontal, which means the spacing of letters and words, or vertical, which deals with space between the lines of writing. Generous spacing in either case denotes a liberal mind and one not given to prejudices. Close, cramped spacing shows a narrow mind.

People who are very frugal and economical show it even in their writing. They use no more space for a word than is necessary, and even cut down the space between words and letters. Extravagant people leave a great deal of space between letters and words.

Practical people rarely leave wide margins on paper, filling most of the available space with legible script. People who are artistic and imaginative often leave wide margins on both sides, preferring a note of beauty and arrangement to complete utility.

People who love luxury and like to revel in the soft, rich things of life leave a great deal of space between lines. Persons who are not so sensitive to luxury or beauty crowd their lines together. An even, regular distance between lines denotes a nature with a sense of fair play. Irregular spacing shows a variable nature.

Capitals

The size and shape of the capitals indicate the writer's opinion of him- or herself, and his or her artistic leanings and appreciations. Size is an index of self-importance, and shape of the aesthetic perceptions.

The greater a person's opinion of his or her own worth and importance, especially intellectually, the higher the person makes his or her capital letters. When they are of average height, they indicate a proper self-respect. Sometimes, the capitals are three or four times the size of the small letters, indicating a large ego.

If only the first stroke of a capital is raised, it denotes social ambitions. Such people are always trying to get on fashionable committees, and love to see their names mentioned in connection with celebrities. When the last stroke of the capital is raised, so that it stands out, it indicates complete self-satisfaction. Men and women who have made a success of their careers often indulge in this sign.

When capitals are written narrow at the base, and wide at the top, the writer is a skeptic. It is hard to make this person believe anything until he or she has seen all the possible evidence you can muster. When the capitals are wide at the base and narrow at the top, the writer is more credulous and will accept much upon faith, not bothering to inquire into the veracity of everything.

Capitals furnish a real opportunity for adornment and expansion. Gracefully written capitals denote an artistic feeling, a love of harmony and symmetry in the home and in personal apparel. Printed capitals indicate a love of form.

When capitals are formed merely by enlarging small letters instead of taking the trouble to write them in their conventional form, it indicates a simple nature, with an elementary taste. Ungraceful and complicated capitals that look like miniature labyrinths are usually an indication of showy natures inclined to boasting and vulgar display.

Endings

The endings, or the final strokes on words, offer a wide range of elements for the interpretation of peculiar characteristics. Their various lengths, shapes, and positions shed new light on the nature and temperament of the writer.

When the final stroke on a word is long, it denotes a generous nature. Such a person will not stint either time or money to help another. When there are no final strokes at all, it indicates a selfish nature, and one engrossed wholly in personal advancement.

Some final strokes, however, like those on the letters *a*, *c*, and *e*, which are easily drawn out, do not necessarily indicate generosity. When final strokes are used to fill otherwise blank spaces, particularly at the end of lines, it denotes a suspicious nature, as though the writer was prolonging each stroke to prevent someone from tampering or filling in on his script.

Tiny upsurges at the termination of final strokes, resembling a face in laughter, show a warm, humorous nature, one that likes to laugh and to provoke laughter. When the final strokes are turned down, it denotes a practical, matter-of-fact nature.

33 Ways to Tell Your Future

A concave stroke at the end of the word denotes a versatile nature. When the end stroke extends upward to the right, it denotes a courageous nature. When it goes down to the right, it shows a timid person. When the terminal strokes go up vertically, they show a writer who loves the secretive and mysterious, and when they go down vertically, they denote a person who is afraid of the unknown.

Terminal strokes that curl under a word, almost like a protecting arm, show a strong paternal or maternal instinct. Such writers make devoted parents.

Punctuation

A person who uses punctuation marks very meticulously, never omitting one, to help clarify his or her expressions, can be characterized as one who is very careful and watchful in life. One who neglects them has a careless nature; this is the type of person who dresses slovenly, comes late to an appointment, and leaves important papers at home.

A person who emphasizes periods so that they almost resemble dashes has a great deal of caution. A round, deliberate dot shows a placid, calm temperament, while quickly made, elongated dots show a disturbed, excitable nature.

When the page is decorated with underscored words, and there are numerous exclamation marks and quotation marks, the writer is a person with a romantic nature and a love of intrigue.

Flourishes

A flourish is a decorative sign made usually by way of ostentation. All those little extra strokes, not necessary for clarity in writing, but made purely for effect, or to express an individual temperament, are flourishes.

A complete absence of flourishes indicates a modest, retiring nature. Most people, during some moods of expansion, indulge in a flourish or two. Therefore, a liberal specimen of writing must be considered before a judgment is reached.

When the beginning strokes are flourished, it denotes a love of ceremony and pomp. Such persons stand very much on their dignity and on the order of things.

A flourish at the end of sentences or paragraphs shows an egotistical nature, and one certain of having put over a particular point very ably. It is also the mark of amateur writers who indulge in overworked passages in letters to admiring friends or to doting mothers. Usually, however, the degree of ostentation in a person can be determined by the exuberance and frequency of their flourishes.

General Point

A strong, dominant person will always guide his or her pen firmly across the page. A weak, indifferent person, insecure in his or her own ability, will write a feeble script.

There are some people whose writing never seems to vary. No matter what the occasion, and how much time has elapsed since the last specimen, their handwriting is the same. These are stolid, matter-of-fact people who never show the stress of emergency or the passage of the years.

People whose writing is never "twice alike" usually have characters that are unformed, or not of decided temperament. When they are still young, there is hope for a mature formation of character. But for people older than thirty-five, a handwriting that changes from line to line shows a definitely changeable nature that is as much trouble for them as it is for those who know them.

The neatness of a page in general is a clue to the meticulousness of the writer. A page that is scrawled, strewn with stray pen marks, or carelessly spaced shows a sloppy, negligent person.

Any very distinctive style in writing shows an original streak in the person. When this is carried to an extreme with very unusual signs, it denotes a person who is eccentric and who will go to any extent to be different from others.

A smooth, running hand shows an easy, unencumbered mind. Fluency of thought and expression is often coupled with ease in writing. The even swing of words shows a sense of rhythm and harmony.

When a person makes the same letter the same way throughout a given specimen of writing, it shows a consistent nature. A continual variation shows a restless trait and a love of change. An absent letter in a word is explained by either haste or absentmindedness, except, of course, in those cases where ignorance of the language produces

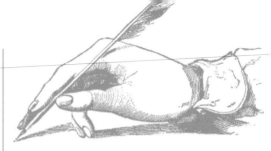

errors in spelling. If it is haste, the writing will show it in the rapid formation of the words and in the half-formed letters. If it is absentmindedness, it will be a very obvious omission and usually repeated.

When there is a tendency to loop the *t*'s and *d*'s, the person is usually quite talkative, and when the loops are quite round, the person is fond of flattery. When *t*'s and *d*'s are quite pointed at the top, the writer is secretive and dislikes talk. When the *i*'s are carefully dotted, it denotes an unusually good memory, as most people forget to dot them and then return to correct this omission. When the *m*'s and *n*'s resemble the *u*'s and *w*'s, as is frequently found, the writer is versatile and can readily adapt to a new set of conditions.

When the stem of the letter *p* is short above the line but continues long below the line, it is a sign of physical strength. When its lower point is sharp and the upstroke is to the right of the stem, it signifies aggressiveness. When the cross stroke is drawn to the right of the stem in the letter *t*, it denotes an impulsive nature. Mild-mannered people usually cross the *t* very low. People of fierce natures cross it very high.

Handwriting Exercises

17

Your Opposite Hand Can't Lie

Here is another way of reading handwriting—read one's character from opposite-hand handwriting! Most people can cultivate a style of writing with their dominant hand, but with the other hand this is not usual. So handwriting made with the nondominant hand should show a natural outline. Have everyone whose handwriting you're analyzing write some copy with their nondominant hand. Ask them all to write the word *Love*. You can get their character from the meanings below.

love   Love   Love   Love   Love   Love   Love

Should individuals write the letters of the word rather close together, it shows that they have a very fine nature and like to do everything precisely. They can always be counted on in an emergency and should always have a good share of happiness and good fortune in life.

The wide spacing of this word shows that these writers have a very generous nature. They will never be so happy as when they have someone to love and nurture. Few people will have a word to say against them, and they should get on well in life.

Very thick writing denotes that these individuals have a strong will, but very fair judgment. Anyone can go to them when worried and be sure to find comfort and understanding. These individuals will make very good mates and will run the household very successfully. There is one thing they should guard against—being too self-sacrificing.

Individuals with thin writing are inclined to belittle themselves. They should try to assert themselves, for they have the makings of being very successful and popular. Children and dogs will always like them, and they will be happier when in the company of either. They will do anything for their friends.

People who write the word legibly but with no special characteristics will always be happy. They can take the rough with the smooth. They always look for the best in everyone, and because of this they will always have friends. Partnerships will be very happy.

People who write the word so that it is scarcely legible have a worrying nature. They are true friends at all times and can be trusted to keep their counsel if asked to. These people will have many unexpected pieces of luck about money in their lives.

Writing that slopes forward all the time belongs to people who like to get the most out of life, and share their good fortune with those they care about. They have honest dispositions and will always be popular. These are individuals who will never let themselves become wallflowers.

Writing that slopes backward belongs to people who have rather a timid nature. They are inclined to hang back instead of pushing forward. They will always have many admirers. There is a good possibility, too, that women will play a big part in bringing these individuals' sweethearts to them.

Straight-up-and-down writing that does not slope either to the right or to the left belongs to the finest type of people going. These individuals are true, levelheaded, kindhearted, and generous. They will have much happiness in their lives and will succeed in their ambitions. They can look forward to making new friends under very romantic circumstances.

Individuals whose writing slopes upward make very fine friends. They have an optimistic outlook on life. There is only one thing that they should guard against, and that is a slight quickness of temper. If they overcome this failing, they will have a very successful life.

Writing that slopes downward all the way belongs to people who are inclined to be easily depressed or let down. They have such kind hearts that things affect them more than they do most people. There will be few very close friends in their lives, but they will all be very faithful. Married life will probably be the happiest years.

Writing that runs straight across from right to left shows very levelheaded people. They can face all sorts of worries and troubles and see a way out of them. They will always be a favorite with their own relatives and friends. There is only one thing for them to guard against in life, and that is taking risks with health. They should try to avoid chills at all costs.

Writing that slopes downward, then upward, describes individuals who are inclined to change their minds often. But kindness of heart will always bring them many loyal companions.

Let Your Guardian Spirit Guide You

This simple exercise can be quite revealing. Have everyone sit around a table, and give each person a sheet of paper and a pencil. Give them ten seconds to clear their minds, and then instruct them to hold their pencils just above the paper and let their guardian spirits guide their hands to make any marks, lines, or shapes they wish to make.

Here is a list of the most common signs drawn, with their meanings. If any of the guests draw any other signs, you can adapt the readings from the ones given here.

A dot means that the writer is very practical and can concentrate very hard. He or she should be very successful in business but should guard against a tendency to ruthlessness.

A small stroke shows that the writer is very levelheaded and can be counted on to give a fair judgment on any problem. This person should make a good friend.

A few disorganized dots show that the person is easily distracted and must keep a better grip on him- or herself.

A small number of tiny disorganized lines show that the writer has a strong sense of what's right. He or she should guard against being too assertive but will always have many friends.

One or more lines all joined at sharp angles show that the writer has a strong personality and a quick mind. To be really successful, however, this individual should try to concentrate on one subject at a time.

A series of curves show that the person has a kind and loving nature and tries at all costs to keep peace. He or she will always have friends but should avoid being put upon.

A complete circle belongs to a person with a mind that gets a fixed view on an idea and will not change it for anyone. This person should guard against being too stubborn, or people will avoid him or her.

A **complete oblong** represents a man or woman with very fine qualities. This person will be successful in business and will never attempt to cheat anyone. His or her life should be a happy one.

A **figure with every angle sharp** also shows the writer to be of an upright character. But this one would be well-advised to concentrate more on his or her ambitions. Success should follow if he or she does.

A **rectangle and curve combined** show that the writer is of a kind nature and will always have moderate prosperity and quite nice friends. The worries of life will come, but they will always go.

A **series of straight lines and curves all pointing upward** is a very good sign. This belongs to a person with a fine nature. He or she will love children and animals and is generous. He or she will never lack friends.

A **series of lines and curves pointing both upward and downward** shows a tendency to a weak will. The owner of this sign should try to cultivate a little more assertiveness and refuse to be put upon.

A **series of lines joined and one disjoined** is a sign that the owner will never lack courage to stand up for his or her convictions. Life may treat this individual hardly at times, but he or she should almost always come up on top.

A **series of lines with a separate curve** shows strong character, with a trace of weakness where children are concerned. This person should guard against being too indulgent to them. Money will slip through this person's fingers, but he or she will nearly always be happy.

A **circle within a circle** represents a person who thinks too little of him- or herself. This individual will be thought far more of if he or she is not so obliging and willing and lets other people do the unpleasant jobs for a change.

A **dot in an irregular figure** represents a person who has a strong idea of his or her own importance. This person should guard against being offensively egotistical.

A **dot and a line together** show a person who is levelheaded in business and yet inclined to be very romantic.

33 Ways to Tell Your Future

Crystal Gazing

18

One of the most interesting and mysterious ways of foretelling the future is by means of the crystal. Those adept at crystal gazing are called "seers," as in "those who see." You may have the gift. No one can say whether you or someone you know has it or not until you have given it a good trial to see what results you get. If the gift is dormant, practice and self-training will bring it out and strengthen it.

Not everyone has the ability to see visions in the crystal. Those few who do, by practicing, can often get really wonderful results. As we have said, only by experiment can you be sure whether you can become a crystal gazer or not, for it is never possible to say beforehand exactly who has the gift.

Certain qualifications are, of course, essential to the most successful seer, the most important being intuition. Another is cleverness in quick interpretation, and another is what we call "the inward eye," which sees the complete vision even while it is yet taking form.

Crystal Gazing

How to Practice Crystal Gazing

There is a definite technique for seeing visions in the crystal sphere, and you must obey certain simple rules before you can even hope for success. The crystal is a beautiful thing in itself, being of quartz or beryl, occasionally ovate in shape but more often round. There are two ways of placing the gleaming globe. It is sometimes held in the left palm of the seer, but generally it is set on a stand, on a square of black material, preferably velvet, all of which is on a table.

In order that the crystal and the vision it is to bring forth may be clear and distinct, dark cloth should be hung in the immediate background or placed under it. This also aids in concentration. Remember that complete silence should be maintained while waiting for the visions to take form within the sphere.

Sit with your back to the light, in a room that, without being at all dark, is what we might call shady. You should be able to see to read in it, but there must not be bright light anywhere, either daylight or artificial. In the daytime a room that faces north is best.

The other people in the room must sit at least an arm's length away from you, the seer—farther than that is better. If they ask you questions during the sitting, they should use an expressionless, monotonous voice, all in one note, as this will not startle you or distract your attention from the crystal.

Apart from any necessary questions or anything you may describe, there must be total silence during a sitting, which at first should not last longer than a quarter of an hour, so that a regular habit is established. If possible, the same people should always be present.

Unless there is an unusual closeness between them, only two should be present besides you, and these should be people who are sympathetic toward crystal gazing, toward you, and toward each other, so that there is no disharmony in the atmosphere.

You must look steadily into the crystal all through the sitting, ignoring your surroundings and trying to let your mind wander as it will. Do not concentrate; in fact, do the exact opposite, opening your mind to whatever chooses to come in. Forget yourself and all your affairs. These things are not easy to accomplish, but to the right type of person they become simple with practice.

It is quite likely that at the first few sittings you will get no results at all. But if you are a natural-born seer, one day the moment will come when the "picture" in the crystal is about to appear. You will first see the clear gleam of the ball begin to turn opaque. It looks like a sphere of gently swirling milk. This in turn can give way to many glowing colors, which at length disappear while the whole crystal appears black. Then comes the thrilling moment when the blackness dissolves like a curtain that is pulled aside, and you see a living picture in the crystal—a picture your intuition will enable you to interpret to your sitters. It is then that you must use the utmost self-control and intelligence, so that you may correctly interpret the vision to the listener.

Remember when you get to the stage of seeing visions that they may be of two kinds—events that appear to you vividly in every detail or symbolic pictures that have to be interpreted. In the second case, the actual picture does not matter; it is its meaning that you must seek and translate. If sitters have asked for information on definite questions, the answers will most often come in this way.

It is impossible to give a list of symbols and their meanings, as in dream interpretation, for with the crystal so much depends upon the individual seer. The meaning is generally grasped by the seer's own psychic sense. In general, a symbol must be interpreted according to its nature and the uses to which it is put.

For example, a ship can denote voyages or the interaction between people at a distance. The Sun, brightly shining, means prosperity and honor; the crescent Moon, which is soon to become bigger, stands, therefore, for increase of success or improvement of some kind. You would naturally know that a foot would indicate taking a step forward; a mouth, an important statement or possibly gossip; an ear, an admonition to listen for news or information; and so on. A bright jewel would indicate riches and importance; a coin, success and monetary gain.

The crystal is, after all, only the medium that both diffuses your ordinary thinking and focuses your attention on your intuition, and so puts you in touch with the unseen world. As a professional psychic, I have trained myself to visit the unseen world at will. Crystal gazing can help you become psychic, too. What you "see" in the crystal you must bring back in your own fashion to those who are sitting with you, translating the symbols into language that they will understand and not relying on a cut-and-dried list of meanings.

Consistent effort will often develop the gift that has lain latent, and a person uneducated and completely unversed in things occult may become a brilliant gazer. No two seers interpret the same visions alike. The seer must rely on his or her own gifts when explaining what is revealed in the magic sphere.

Crystal Gazing

wealth & prosperity	fame & reputation	love & relationships
family & friends	health & well-being	creativity & children
knowledge & wisdom	career & life path	helpful people

The relationship between wind and water has been studied by many cultures, most notably that of China, where the ancient practice of feng shui, pronounced "fung shway," which literally means "wind and water," exerts as powerful an influence on the daily lives of modern-day people as it did on their ancestors. Feng shui, which is also known as "the art of placement," concerns itself with the arrangement of all things in harmony with the natural environment and the unseen flow of the great invisible force that supports and sustains all of nature, an energy called "chi."

The principles of feng shui are used today in virtually all aspects of life in China but especially in interior design and decoration. The primary goal is to ensure an unimpeded flow and interplay of chi energy that promotes health, wealth, and good fortune.

The *bagua*, an eight-sided symbol, is the essential feng shui tool used to map out rooms, buildings, and spaces to locate the areas that correspond to various parts of one's life. The size of a space is not as important as the energy condition of the space. It is essential to remember that all positions are figured from the front door of any space, the door through which one enters.

We'd like to address the issue of your main door, the front door of your dwelling, and how important that is in the art of feng shui. You may think of your front door as just the door guests use to enter your home, but for feng shui purposes, your front door is the gateway to positive energy and opportunities! It is one of the most important places in your home.

No matter how many entrances you have in your home, you have only one main, front entrance. Try to use your front door as the way you most often enter your dwelling. Your door should open easily, with nothing impeding it. Your door should not be broken in any way. Your door handle should work smoothly and without unnecessary noise. The inside of your entryway should be well lit.

To overlay the *bagua* on your home or work floor plan, stand at the threshold of the door, facing in, and hold the diagram on page 108 so that the bottom three areas are closest to you.

The following are the nine life areas of the *bagua*:

1. Helpful People—right front
2. Career—center front
3. Knowledge—left front
4. Family—center left
5. Wealth/Money—back left
6. Fame/Reputation—back center
7. Love/Relationships—back right
8. Creativity/Children—center right
9. Health—center

You can apply the *bagua* map to any space, including but not limited to your home, office, cubicle, or any individual area. By turning our attention to and enhancing these areas, we can create positive results in our lives. When the *bagua* pattern is placed over the floor plan of a room or building, it pinpoints the specific areas that influence these nine key aspects. You can then place a wind chime in the relevant locations to enhance those areas of your life.

Using the *bagua* placement system, stand in the doorway you use most to enter your room or office, and locate the nine different zones that make up the *bagua* and the specific life situations associated with them (as in the *bagua* map illustration). Before you hang up your wind chime, you may want to read all of the descriptions and affirmations below to help to guide you to the most important area of your life to enhance right now.

1. Helpful People and Travel

Hang your wind chime in this corner of your home or office if you would like the universe to send you help to make your life easier, either in the form of helpful people and circumstances, or as the opportunity to rest and rejuvenate through enjoyable travel. Place globes, maps, and pictures of places you have visited or would like to visit in this area.

2. Career and Life Path

Hang your wind chime in this corner of your home or office if you would like to discover what you should be doing with your life or have clarity and fulfillment regarding your job or career. This part of your room or home is the best place to display awards you've won or would like to win and to place your home office and computer.

3. Knowledge and Wisdom

Hang your wind chime in this corner of your home or office when you want to increase your knowledge about any subject and gain wisdom from doing so—remember that they're not the same thing. This is the area of your room to enhance with related objects and images if you are in school or if you are a businessperson working on deal making, systems design, information processing, or computer networks. This is the perfect spot for a bookshelf and reading area.

4. Family and Friends

Hang your wind chime in this corner of your home or office when you want to increase the harmonious interaction between you and your family and friends. This is the area of your room to hang your wind chime if you would like to attract beneficial friendships or cure misunderstandings between you and family, friends, or neighbors. Place mementos and photos of beloved ancestors and those you care about.

5. Wealth and Prosperity

Hang your wind chime in this corner of your home or office if you would like wealth, prosperity, and power to flow to you and your endeavors. Adding one or more bright lights and beautiful plants to this corner will light your way to growth and happiness as you learn what true wealth, prosperity, and power really are.

6. Fame and Reputation

Hang your wind chime in this corner of your home or office if you would like to improve how you, your efforts, or both are perceived by other people. This area of your room represents your goals, so also place objects, photographs, and other images there that symbolize your aspirations and dreams.

7. Love and Relationships

Hang your wind chime in this corner of your home or office if you would like to find love or improve an existing relationship. This area encompasses close relationships, such as husband and wife, business partnerships, and very intimate friendships. Hanging the wind chime here can also help you to feel content and fulfilled with current relationships. If possible, this area of your home would be a great place for a romantic bedroom. Decorate it with green and pink colors, representing mutual growth and love.

8. Creativity and Children

Hang your wind chime in this corner of your home or office if you would like to express yourself more creatively and bring something new to life. This area also represents children, new projects, or hobbies. Also, if you are feeling burned out or bored, or having trouble conceiving or relating to your children, enhance this area with objects and images that represent the positive aspects of children, creativity, and creative people.

9. Health and Well-Being

Hang your wind chime in the center of your home or office when you want to maintain the best level of health of which you are capable and the patience, understanding, and contentment necessary to deal with all challenges. Since this area lies in the middle of the *bagua*/room/home, it touches all other areas and helps cure all other life situations not mentioned above. Hang your wind chime here to enhance your sense of well-being.

Some Essential Feng Shui Tips

Once you accept the connection between the physical action of conscious placement and arrangement and the harmonious flow of chi through the various areas of your life, you are well on your way to improving your life. Changing your mind-set and remembering your intention help you attain your goals. Believing that something good will come to you helps you to keep your eyes open so you will notice that great opportunity when it comes your way.

However, there are other easy things you can do to help you make your desired improvements in your life, unimpeded by what we call the "enemies" of feng shui. Here are some important feng shui tips, which are essential for anyone wanting to add some positive energy to their lives:

1. Make it a practice to remove your shoes before or upon entering your home.

2. Clear all clutter from every area of your living space that's under your control.

3. Fix all leaks, from water pipes to faucets to roofs.

4. Make sure your stove is in good working order, and use it to cook as often as you can.

5. Add trees, plants, or upward lighting to raise energy. Dispose of dead plants inside your dwelling space and in areas outside your home that you are responsible for.

6. Keep your toilet seat closed when not in use, especially when flushing, to avoid flushing away good chi. This sounds odd, but it is one of the most widely practiced feng shui techniques we know of.

7. Only if it is safe and practical, open your windows for at least twenty minutes a day to allow fresh chi to come in.

8. Replace any and all dead lightbulbs with working ones.

9. There should be no television sets in any bedroom (sorry, but it's a big feng shui no-no!).

10. Arrange furniture so you can face the doors while sitting (or add a mirror so you can see behind you). Avoid sitting with your back to a door if you can.

11. Oil your doors' hinges so they don't squeak, reducing mental irritation.

12. Add color or art throughout your home to bring in desired positive energy.

Automatic Writing

20

Automatic writing is a simple procedure. Whether you are interested in channeling spirit entities or your own subconscious mind, automatic writing requires no special skills on your part, with the exception of patience and concentration.

If you truly wish to have accurate communication with the spiritual entities of those who have passed over, it is important to maintain a cool, dispassionate demeanor and a balance between being open-minded and being practical. In other words, you should open yourself up to the experience but avoid taking directions from any spirit entity you contact. Naturally, this means that you are still responsible for checking out any information that comes to you from the other side; it's research, not gospel.

You may receive amazing information that seems one hundred percent true. Even so, approach your sessions as research to be studied and evaluated, and no more. You should not follow directions or take advice from anyone without being logical, prudent, and careful. So long as you follow this recommendation, you will have a good experience.

It should be pointed out that channeling is really no different or more difficult than concentrating on emptying your mind of deliberate influences. By distinguishing between external thoughts and your Higher Self, you will be able to keep from influencing the written messages that you receive.

Believe it or not, some people unconsciously block spirit communication, either because they fear it or, conversely, because they want so badly to make it happen. Often, even when we think we are not deliberately influencing our actions through thought, we can be. This is something that must be curbed when you attempt to channel. Even if it is a problem for you at first, you will learn the correct method through repetition.

An Automatic Writing Session

In order to have a successful experience, it is important to adhere to the following procedure and guidelines as closely as possible, though you may certainly make minor changes and eventually mold them to your individual style. Remember, you are in control. If for some reason you want to stop the session at any time, you are free to do so. It is important that you give yourself this permission before you begin.

1. Plan your session for when you are free from distractions and there are no other immediate demands on your time. Don't attempt to do a session if you have to dash off to work or to an appointment in an hour or so. Even if you think you have enough time before your appointment to conduct the session, you may subconsciously rush the endeavor, which can result in failure.

2. Place a legal-size (or even larger) pad or piece of paper on a table or on a tray you can hold on your lap. If you don't have a suitable table or tray, you can try using a piece of clean, rigid cardboard that is perfectly smooth and seamless. You may want to use masking tape to adhere your large blank piece of paper to the table or tray. The goal is to stabilize your writing area because you might encounter a spirit with a lot of energy and the planchette could start moving around vigorously!

3. If you are using a table, sit on a chair that is high enough so that your arms and wrists are relaxed and able to comfortably allow the pen in your hand to reach every corner of your piece of paper when you place your fingertips lightly on it. You should feel the same level of relaxation and comfort if you are using a tray or other platform resting on your lap.

4. Before you begin, make sure to write the date at the top of the page. This will be helpful when you want to check your notes for accuracy and to reawaken your own memory at some later date.

5. Relax. Get comfortable. You should always center yourself emotionally and spiritually before you begin. We strongly advise you to say a prayer for psychic protection prior to your session. It is also a good idea to first visualize yourself surrounded by a cone of white light. This acts as a barrier between you and any unwholesome influence caused by your own fears and prejudices that could possibly come through during the session.

6. Once you have performed your protection ritual, close your eyes and allow your whole body to relax. Breathe deeply and exhale three times. Each time you breathe in, feel the inspiring power of All There Is merging with your own personal power. Each time you breathe out, tell yourself that this is going to be a positive experience. Do not tense your hand. Be aware of any sense of stress leaving your neck, your shoulders, your arms and hands. This signals that you are moving into a semitrance state and are now ready to receive messages. The simple act of closing your eyes and concentrating on your breath slows brain activity from its usual beta-wave state down to where it is generating alpha waves, a state that is perfectly sufficient for engaging in automatic writing.

7. Automatic writing should be just that—automatic. The goal of putting yourself into the state of relaxed concentration that produces alpha brain waves is to enable you to "get out of your own way" and let the energies that are going to move your pen do their work without your interference. The messages are supposed to come either from your subconscious mind or from a spirit entity, and once you've prepared yourself properly, as described above, you can start your pen moving in a small circle or a figure eight, the signs for infinity.

8. Request to speak to one of your spirit guides. You should do this aloud because, as stated above, you should be leaving your mind open. Do not be embarrassed or distracted by the sound of your voice. Speak clearly and distinctly. Tell the spirit guide you wish him

or her to communicate with you through the method of automatic writing. The spirit guide has to adjust to the process as much as you do, so consider yourself part of a team.

9. When you are first learning, ask questions that can be answered by a *y* or 1 for *yes* or an *n* or 2, or even just two vertical lines, for *no*. Do not expect to have clearly legible printing or flowing script pour from your pen until you are completely comfortable with the process.

10. Then mentally let go of your control of the pen and allow your hand to continue to move it, but without your conscious direction. This sounds tricky to accomplish, and it sometimes is, at first. But after a few tries, you should see results of an ever-improving nature. It is going to look and feel like you are moving the pen yourself, for you are certainly supplying part of the energy to move it—but not all of it.

Have faith that benign forces are trying to contact you, and see what happens. Try not to have any preconceived ideas or notions about what it is going to write when you feel the pen's movements under your hand. Let the pen begin to write or draw as if a spirit was working with you. Try to keep a gentle pressure on the pen—allow it to move freely, but hold it securely enough to keep it touching the paper.

11. Do not stop to read what you have written. Simply let it flow! Do not be frightened or overwhelmed by emotion. You may feel a surge of power move through your hand as you write.

12. Once you get the feel of automatic writing, you can start asking more detailed questions whose answers will be limited only by the size of your piece of paper. You should use your own words, but you might want to phrase your questions something like this: "Spirit guides, could you come and talk to me? I open my heart and my mind to what you have to say. Who is here? What was your name when you lived in my world?" Keep your questions general at first, before you start asking specific questions about yourself. Once you are familiar with the process, you can say, "I have a problem that I need an answer to; could you please come and talk to me about it?"

13. If nothing happens at first, don't be disappointed or upset. Repeat your request, and then empty your mind of all extraneous thoughts and feelings. Continue to breathe deeply. Then say aloud, "Spirits, tell me what I need to know." When you feel the tingling sensation of a spirit coming through to you, ask his or her name. This is an important part of the process that must be repeated whenever you do automatic writing. You should always ask a spirit to identify him- or herself.

14. Patience is essential. Some spirits are as excited to speak to us as we are anxious to contact them. Although asking questions about a time period they resided in is perfectly acceptable, avoid asking for anything too specific, such as a particular time or date, as they may have problems with timing. Time is the most difficult prediction, as it doesn't mean the same thing in the spirit realm as it does here on Earth. Be considerate of both the other participants (if you are working with another person) and the spirits.

15. If you believe that several spirits are present, tell them you can speak to only one of them at a time. Stop the session if any of the replies to your questions make you feel uncomfortable. If you ask a question and get not a response to it but an answer that doesn't seem to relate to your question, wait until the next session to ask it again.

16. When you are first beginning, you should not practice automatic writing for more than five to fifteen minutes at a time. When you feel that amount of time has passed, thank the spirit or spirits aloud for their help in guiding you. Count to three, and then allow yourself to come back to total consciousness, feeling wonderful and inspired. As your skills improve, you can gradually lengthen your sessions.

17. After the session is the time to review the writing and/or drawings you created. At first, the messages, symbols, and drawings may not make a lot of sense to you. The writing may be hard to read, and there may not be spaces between the words. Different spirits will have different "handwriting," just as we in this world do. But as you continue to develop your skills, you will become better at interpreting the messages, advice, and all the general information that comes through during each session. As with anything, practice makes perfect. Remember, you will never learn all that you want to in just a few sessions.

18. This is a process that is likely to take place over a prolonged period of time. Much as in dream interpretation, a single dream may mean very little, but taken over time, a whole series of dreams can turn out to be quite enlightening. So it is with automatic writing and drawing. Once you begin to study the writings you have channeled over a period of time, they will have a great deal more significance and meaning to you.

19. Be sure that you thank your spirit guide and the other spirits who helped this information flow in your direction. You must do this aloud, saying something like, "Thank you, kind spirits"—do not forget to include their names if they have been revealed to you—"for sharing your wisdom and advice with me. I hope that you will come and talk with me again on" and give a date and time or just say "next time."

If you end each session in a similar fashion, you will quickly discover that the spirits are more than willing to come back to help you time and time again.

A Word about Spirit Guides

Some people call their personal spirit guides "guardian angels." Others call them "guiding angels." We all have at least one—usually more than one. Sometimes a guide will be a personal friend or loved one we knew in life who has since passed over to the other side. At other times it is a fully nonhuman entity that was created as an angel and has never lived on Earth.

Don't even consider asking your spirit guides to give you tips about stocks, lottery numbers, or the races. In the first place, the practice of channeling is not supposed to be about material matters. It is a spiritual exercise that can bring wisdom and esoteric knowledge into your life. Second, spirit guides are notoriously useless when it comes to material matters.

Do not expect that the same spirit or spirits will always come through; there may be many. As you evolve your communication skills, however, you will develop special relationships with spirit entities with the help of your spirit guide.

Do not be surprised if one or more of your spirit guides exhibits a lightly teasing or humorous quality in your sessions. Often, spirit entities are amused by the serious tone and attitude of those who are still earthbound, and as a result they attempt to inject a bit of levity into the situation. This should not be regarded as a joke being played on you by the spirit entity. It is simply your guiding angel's way of lightening the mood. You must never assume that spirits have no sense of humor, because they do!

You may even be one of those "lucky" people who find a whole gang of departed family members clustered around you, waiting to come through in your first automatic writing session. However, you should also know that for most of us, automatic writing is something that has to be worked at and practiced before it is likely to be successful. Don't let this stop you from pursuing it, though. Be assured that this experience is worth the time and the effort you put into it.

Lucky Color

21

Color is a powerful force, the visible manifestation of atomic vibration and energy absorption. Using color properly can improve your appearance, your home life, and your place of business. The right color promotes the vibrations that can enhance moods, set the tone for meetings of all kind, and accent natural beauty in a number of magical ways. Without color the world is a drab place, indeed. With it, all things are possible.

Which is your lucky color? If you know it, that's great! Make use of it in every possible way. When wearing fashions made of it, you will be more confident in yourself than when arrayed in something else. You will get more work done, and it will be better work.

Not only should you wear your fortunate color, but it is a good plan to surround yourself with it. We know a woman whose dresses are mostly purple; the wallpaper in her bedroom is purple; purple casement curtains adorn the windows; there are purple rugs in various parts of the house; even the back of the hairbrush on her dressing table is purple. And, since she decided that purple was her lucky color, and used it in every reasonable way, she has had several strokes of marvelous good fortune. You must be sure, however, that it is your lucky color. If you are not quite sure, then read on.

Of course, you may say in reply to all this that you do not know your lucky color. What then? This is where we can give you a little help. Most people's lucky color depends on the time of their birth. The following list sets out the birth colors.

We know full well that everybody does not derive good fortune from their birth color, but that they find it in some other hue. Therefore, the proper course is to make trials with the appropriate color listed below and, if that does not answer satisfactorily, to choose another of your own liking and try that. Only by personal experiment can you finally decide.

These are the birth colors. The first given for any period is the one almost universally accepted. Those following after the first are, however, favored by a certain number of people.

December 22–January 20	Emerald green, sapphire blue, and black
January 21–February 19	Various blues and dark green
February 20–March 20	Purple, white, and silver
March 21–April 19	Rose red, other shades of red
April 20–May 20	Turquoise blue, other shades of blue
May 21–June 21	Light shades of yellow, orange, and gold
June 22–July 22	Mauve, white, and silver
July 23–August 21	Gold, brown, and yellow
August 22–September 22	Yellow, orange, and light blue
September 23–October 23	Rose pink and yellow
October 24–November 22	Dark green, red, and brown
November 23–December 21	Purple and blue

Colors, of course, have certain values attached to them. Meditate upon the color whose energies, as described below, are what you are looking to manifest in your life today. Clear your mind, take a few deep breaths, and stare at an object in the color you have chosen. Breathe in the color until you can feel it seep into your skin and deep inside you. Repeat this ritual whenever you feel as if you need a psychic "color infusion" in order to bring strength, happiness, prosperity, or any other good thing into your life.

Red

Red signifies confidence and courage. It inspires boldness in thought and deed. A strong awareness of the physical body is indicated. There can sometimes be so much passion in its energy that when it is displayed it can be perceived as aggression.

Fuchsia

The color fuchsia can influence both physical and spiritual well-being. It is the flag for nonconformist, innovative, strong-willed, imaginative, artistic, and creative individuals. Depending on how it is received, it can be the color of radiant happiness.

Orange

Orange is a joyous color, representing vibrant energy and intellectual curiosity. It is the color of surprise and enthusiasm. It promotes physical attraction as well as friendship. It has a sense of humor; wearing a bit of orange can bring smiles and a sense of optimism.

Yellow

The color yellow signifies cheerfulness, optimism, and bright ideas. It is a happy and energetic color that reflects mental acuity and communication. It is also a celebration of sunny days. Yellow energy is related to the ability to perceive and understand.

Green

Green is one of the colors that best reflects both the magical and the material world. In the material sense it represents employment, money, prosperity, and success. In the magical sense it symbolizes fertility, healing, growth, and the good, green Earth.

Blue

Blue symbolizes peace and emotional tranquility. It also inspires mental control, creativity, and clarity. Blue has pacifying effect. It symbolizes the sky, the shielding dome above our heads, and therefore represents boundless potential and opportunities.

Aqua

Aqua is a serene yet uplifting color. Aqua promotes clear communication, honesty, openness, and the need to join together with others. It represents the ability to transform, just as water turns to ice and the cycle repeats.

Purple

Purple denotes power, authority, and psychic strength. In a metaphysical sense, purple energy connects us to our spiritual guidance, wisdom, and inner strength. Purple is a color of transformation, combating fear and resistance to change.

Indigo

Indigo is the color of spiritual awakening and awareness. It is an imaginative, intuitive, and mystical shade. It inspires sensitivity to beauty, harmony, and compassion for others, as well as promoting lucid dreams and dream skills such as problem solving.

Brown

Brown is the ultimate earth tone, reflective of nature, especially in the autumnal months. It can be a stabilizing influence both psychologically and emotionally. It denotes practicality, simplicity, humility, and purposefulness.

Lucky Color

Lavender

Lavender is the color of spiritual healing, dispelling sadness, loneliness, and mental confusion. It is helpful in opening the third eye. It can also reflect romance and sentimentality and is a good color for use on the walls of a place where meditation is practiced.

Pink

Pink is the color of joy and personal happiness. This lively yet gentle shade reflects optimism, a youthful attitude, and the ability to take chances. It signifies romantic rather than sexual love. It has the ability to bring a fresh perspective to any endeavor.

Black

Black is not actually a color but the absence of color. It can be off-putting because of its intensity, but it is actually comforting, protective, and mysterious. It is good for banishing negativity, absorbing negativity, or fighting negativity from an outside source.

Tan

Classic and understated, tan suggests the path of moderation, relaxation, undemanding energy, and neutrality. While it may be seen as representing a conservative attitude, its energy signifies dependability, caring, and common sense.

Gray

Gray represents the middle ground, neither completely positive nor completely negative. Its energy suggests quiet, emptiness, and lack of movement, yet it has a stabilizing and balancing effect, making vibrant colors stand out while muting their vibration.

White

White is the emblem of innocence, purity, and peace and denotes spiritual authority. It radiates a protective and charismatic energy, which is why it is used by seekers and seers when meditating, as a protective shield or enveloping ball or egg shape of energy.

Candle Gazing

22

Candle gazing is fun, but there are a number of commonsense precautions that must be understood and put into practice before you start. Always be as careful as possible when working with matches and fire—you must take all necessary precautions. Make sure to place any candle or incense to be burned in a stable, fireproof holder that you place safely, in a well-ventilated area, so that its flame cannot be touched accidentally or knocked over by anything, including the wind. Never place a candle anywhere where it is near combustible materials such as, but not limited to, paper or curtains. Never, ever, leave a candle or incense unattended for any reason, not even for a second.

Find a quiet place, free of disturbances—people, phones, pets, fans, or air conditioners—that might disturb the flame. You may use soft background music. Some people enjoy using incense. Wear clothing that is comfortable but not loose enough to accidentally touch the candle's flame.

We prefer large, thick candles that are stable, are hard to knock over, and last for hours. If you so desire, choose an appropriate color candle to go along with the attributes you seek today, as found in the "Lucky Color" chapter on page 119.

The procedure is the same as with all reflecting objects: Clear your mind of all thoughts, listen, and see with your inner self. Awaken the receptive power, and open this world to the next. Visions will come when you are receptive to them. Let them speak.

On a relaxing evening, when you sit gazing half dreamily into the glowing heart of a candle and watching the vague shapes made as the flame flickers, try to see these indefinite pictures more clearly and to interpret them as symbols of what is coming to you in the near future.

Sit in a relatively comfortable chair with the candle approximately an arm's length in front of you—perhaps at a kitchen table. You could also place the candle on a coffee table, then sit on the floor—if you are able to do so without discomfort. Clear and focus your mind on nothing in particular; just keep it open to the symbols as they pass through the flickering flame. Empty all thoughts, and gaze upon the flame and be open to psychic messages that transpire.

This can be a method of self-hypnosis. You can state your intention before you begin focusing on the flame of the candle—for example, "I want to see myself in a past life that links to this one." Now gaze at the flame. Look at the flame. Breathe deeply and evenly, in through your nose and slowly out through your mouth. As you look at the flame, you can see that it is actually made of the colors of the rainbow. Subtle shades of red glow at the very tip of the flame. Your passion, your physical body, are being left behind, as a faint reminder of who you are. The orange that follows spans a short time on the flame.

Then, the yellow, the most prevalent, the most powerful part of the flame, draws your attention. It burns as your creativity, yearning to burst free and shower you with its inspirations. Your eyes follow down and see the tiny segment of green, your center, your growth. This is where the bountiful harvest of your life lies. Feel the growth and abundance everywhere in the universe before you fall into the blue at the base of the flame. The blue, the higher emotion of your secret self,

burns brightly if only you look at it. Below it, barely perceptible, is the violet of your spirit. This is the same spirit that resides within you, but it is barely perceptible day to day.

As you watch your flame/spirit, let the violet flame enlarge and envelop the blue, green, yellow, orange, and red of the fire. Let your spirit enlarge to fill you in the same way. As you inhale, feel your spirit fill you with the light of the candle. Imagine that you are breathing in the beautiful colors of the flame. I also suggest that you refer to the chapter "Teacup Fortune-Telling" on page 11. The symbols described therein can be used as a basic guide for the symbols that you see within the flame.

It may happen that however long you gaze into the flame, you can see nothing clearly, but only vague shapes that convey no meaning to you. When this occurs, you may know that your life is in a state of flux at the moment and the future is too vague to be seen. This is not necessarily unfavorable, but only shows that changes are taking place that, so to speak, muddle the picture. Try again in a few days, and you will probably get clearer results. Do not do candle gazing for more than five minutes on any one occasion. Make sure to thoroughly and completely extinguish your candle and any incense before you get up from your candle-gazing session.

33 *Ways to Tell Your Future*

Playing Card Fortunes

23

There is a great universal curiosity about what the future holds in store. It is part of human nature to want to know what tomorrow will bring. Riches, travel to far-off countries, marriage, health wealth, love, and life—all these are in the palm of Destiny. From time immemorial, a simple deck of playing cards has held the answer to all of these perplexing questions. Let us ascertain what the cards have come to mean.

One of the oldest forms, used chiefly by Hungarian and Romanian gypsies, is as follows:

Let the person who is telling the fortune shuffle an ordinary fifty-two-card deck thoroughly. Let the person whose fortune is being ascertained cut the cards. Reshuffle and cut the deck again.

Let the subject select one card and lay it aside facedown. This is known as the Imminent Card. Now there are fifty-one cards in the deck. Let the teller deal these cards in three even piles, arranging them like a triangle.

The teller picks up the first pile and deals the first card faceup. The second is added to the second pile. The third card is dealt faceup on top of the first pile. The fourth is added to the third pile. Thus, every time a card is added to the first pile, another is placed facedown alternately on the second and third piles. When the seventeen cards have been dealt out, nine cards remain in the first pile, from which the fortune will be ascertained by the following symbols. At the end, the card that has been laid aside tells the one thing that is most imminent in the fortune of the subject.

For additional revelations, this process must be repeated until the desired telltale card is turned up.

The cards, as revealed, signify the following:

ACE OF CLUBS: Prosperity and success will come in the business or profession the subject is engaged in.

KING OF CLUBS: Much needed assistance will come from a man in a superior position.

QUEEN OF CLUBS: Aid will come from a woman. If you are a man, this woman will not be the one you love; if you are a woman, the woman who brings aid will be a relative or an associate.

JACK OF CLUBS: An obstacle in the path of the goal, usually a man, or some deed performed by a rival man.

TEN OF CLUBS: An extremely lucky card, bringing unexpected wealth, or good tidings, and mitigating against any bad cards.

NINE OF CLUBS: Beware the displeasure you will cause someone by what you are planning to do.

EIGHT OF CLUBS: A family council recently held with you or about you and denoting anxiety.

SEVEN OF CLUBS: Someone working for your benefit unknown to you; a card of secret loyalty.

SIX OF CLUBS: A union to be completed in the near future; a marriage if you are unwedded, or a profitable partnership in business, if you are already mated.

FIVE OF CLUBS: A card of doubt, advising further deliberation before making a move under consideration.

FOUR OF CLUBS: A brief journey, which will improve your circumstances.

THREE OF CLUBS: Someone is trying to involve you in a risky venture. This card says you need to be more conservative.

TWO OF CLUBS: News is coming soon for you. Whether or not it is favorable will be determined by a later message from the same source.

Diamonds

ACE OF DIAMONDS: A card of great magnetism, with attendant good fortune. Will attract either a person or an event, which will bring a lucky change.

KING OF DIAMONDS: A patriarchal card. The head of a family, or of a business concern; when following a club, indicates he is in a forgiving mood.

QUEEN OF DIAMONDS: A card of flirtatious behavior, either an actual interaction in store, or some mild deceit to be practiced.

JACK OF DIAMONDS: Some person or event will light the way out of darkness.

TEN OF DIAMONDS: Money to be made through speculation or investment.

NINE OF DIAMONDS: A card of revelation. You are concealing your affections for someone in the same house and you are suffering because of this.

EIGHT OF DIAMONDS: You will encounter a friend of childhood and a fast friendship formed.

SEVEN OF DIAMONDS: Travel near water, but not on the open sea.

SIX OF DIAMONDS: News of an advantageous matter will be received, but not directly.

FIVE OF DIAMONDS: A brief downturn from which either you or some dear one will recover.

FOUR OF DIAMONDS: A visit from or to a relative.

THREE OF DIAMONDS: An enjoyable vacation to be spent in the country with a surprise meeting in the offing.

TWO OF DIAMONDS: Some new interest will soon occupy your life—not a person; more likely a study for cultural reasons or for advancement in business.

Hearts

ACE OF HEARTS: A card of expansion. If it follows a diamond, it means that your worldly goods will soon be increased.

KING OF HEARTS: This card ushers in the grand passion of your life. It is the most important messenger Cupid can send.

QUEEN OF HEARTS: A restorer of faith, particularly to women.

JACK OF HEARTS: Someone is tempting the person you love.

TEN OF HEARTS: Means a sudden journey, which will result in complications, either emotional or financial.

NINE OF HEARTS: A troublesome card, unless it follows a club. In any event, restraint is advised.

EIGHT OF HEARTS: This card will bring consolation either for bereavement or for a loss in business.

SEVEN OF HEARTS: If you are a student, it means examinations will be passed. To others, it spells some advancement.

SIX OF HEARTS: A warning that secret vices are being pursued to your detriment.

FIVE OF HEARTS: A change is being contemplated, either of address, or job, or possibly the heart.

FOUR OF HEARTS: Denotes happiness in a family relationship, although not necessarily in the single state.

THREE OF HEARTS: A love triangle with you, destined to wound the heart of someone who does not expect it.

TWO OF HEARTS: True romance may soon be yours. If there's been a quarrel, reconciliation will soon come.

 ## Spades

ACE OF SPADES: A long-nourished ambition coming to realization.

KING OF SPADES: A change in character and habits to be effected through the influence of some new person.

QUEEN OF SPADES: A woman in a relationship to you is rising in power.

JACK OF SPADES: You should take care to avoid being accident-prone.

TEN OF SPADES: A romance is brewing in a rural setting.

NINE OF SPADES: Reverses, financial or of the heart.

EIGHT OF SPADES: Some legal tangle will be unraveled.

SEVEN OF SPADES: Opposition to a plan now forming will come from an unexpected quarter.

SIX OF SPADES: A joyous occasion in which you will share the success of a dear friend.

FIVE OF SPADES: A triumph before an audience. It may be on a stage or at a private gathering.

FOUR OF SPADES: Travel by water with a congenial group.

THREE OF SPADES: Remorse because of haste in an act, which wounded an old friend.

TWO OF SPADES: A mysterious set of circumstances throwing you innocently under a cloud.

This method uses fifty-two different meanings, one for each card of a regular playing card deck. It can just be read out from this book according to the card drawn. This very simple method makes plenty of fun and laughter at a party.

Shuffle and spread the whole deck of fifty-two cards facedown on the table. The reader must close his or her eyes, hold his or her right hand over the heart, and say,

> A reading true I seek to find,
> And take what comes with quiet mind.

Then with the left hand, the reader draws from the spread cards any one he or she likes and shows it, and its rhymed meaning is read by whoever is holding the book. Then the next person takes a turn, after the card drawn has been replaced in the deck and shuffled around so that this particular card cannot be detected.

Here are the rhymes for the whole deck:

Diamond Rhymes

ACE

If this ace should be your gain,
You'll marry one with wealth and brain.

KING

Pleasure and profit come to you
Where Sun is gold and skies are blue.

QUEEN

Fate sometimes breaks and sometimes bends,
But you'll be helped by all your friends.

JACK

Fate has been a mistress stern,
But from today your luck will turn.

TEN

The charming maid who draws the ten
Will wed, but no one knows just when.

NINE

With this nine good luck attends,
And in a week your income mends.

EIGHT

If you're old or in your youth,
Wealth will come from speaking truth.

SEVEN

When mystic seven doth appear,
Strange happenings will soon be here.

SIX

Be on guard, says number six,
'Gainst enemies and crafty tricks.

FIVE

If asked to travel, please say, "No."
'Twon't bring you any luck to go.

FOUR

A holiday that's full of fun
Is coming 'ere a month is done.

THREE

Great honor comes to you and yours
For every good, sufficient cause.

TWO

Whatever pain you have today,
This card will drive it all away.

Heart Rhymes

ACE

Love is near and you will find
A sweetheart loves you for your mind.

KING

Stand still, consider, if you can,
Or you may love a married man.

QUEEN

Take heed, for one you think your friend,
Of happy plans may make an end.

JACK

A new acquaintance you shall meet,
And find his friendship very sweet.

TEN

Did you think love was at an end?
Ah, no! For broken hearts will mend.

NINE

If these nine pips to you appear,
Your wedding day is very near.

EIGHT

Yours is a lucky working life,
Quite free from poverty or strife.

SEVEN

If the seven you obtain,
Be sure you will not love in vain.

SIX

An enemy will show you spite,
But everything will soon come right.

FIVE

Across the sea you're bound to roam,
But if you go, you'll soon come home.

FOUR

From any worries troubling thee,
The next six months will set you free.

THREE

More haste, more speed, is not your fate,
Better to linger and be late.

TWO

With him you love do not act madly,
Or you may soon be feeling badly.

Club Rhymes

ACE

A jolly person, full of mirth,
Within the week shall learn of birth.

KING

An old acquaintance you will see
And be much in his company.

QUEEN

A woman who you thought was fair
Is jealous of you, so be aware.

JACK

Money is coming, so take heed
And use it wisely for your need.

TEN

In work promotion comes to you
Within a month—more money, too.

NINE

Marriage and money—happy twins
Of luck, quite soon your fortune wins.

EIGHT

Your next proposal don't disdain,
Or you may not get one again.

SEVEN

A little loss may come your way.
Don't fret; 'tis only for a day.

Rhyming Card Fortunes

SIX

This six you've drawn will bring you soon
A heart who sets the world in tune.

FIVE

For parenthood your name is cast,
And your first child won't be the last.

FOUR

Work hard if you success would win,
Your lucky time is coming in.

THREE

If now you love with might in vain,
Look further, please, and love again.

TWO

Today you get the answer "No."
Tomorrow it will not be so.

Spade Rhymes

ACE

A disappointment dims your eyes,
But proves a blessing in disguise.

KING

A trusty friend will help you to
Prosper much in all you do.

QUEEN

A jealous woman—please take care!
You'll know her by her curly hair.

JACK

You're thinking this year to be wed.
Please put it off 'til next instead.

TEN

What today is bringing sorrow,
Will bring you happy smiles tomorrow.

NINE

This week your fortune will be fine,
Since you have drawn of spades the nine.

EIGHT

Please change your business methods or
You'll have no one to change them for.

SEVEN

You'll wed and soon, we must declare,
But not with any trousseau fair.

SIX

Take heart of grace, for you will find
Next winter far more to your mind.

FIVE

Try to avoid a bitter strife
Which may impede your happy life.

FOUR

If you insist on your own way,
You'll likely live to rue the day.

THREE

You've surely drawn a lucky spade,
Money's pleasures will not fade.

TWO

Small troubles bring you many a sigh,
But all comes right, then, by and by.

Cupid's Scroll

Ask any question you like, so long as it concerns love or lovers, whether your own or a friend's.

Shut your eyes and turn this book three times, keeping it open at this page. Keep your mind fixed on the question you are going to ask. Then, with your eyes still shut, try to touch one of the figures in the tablet with your finger or a pencil or other pointer. If the pointer falls outside the tablet, there is no reply today. Try again tomorrow. But should the pointer touch one of the figures, turn to the answers, and against the corresponding number you will find your reply.

At first sight, the reply may not seem to fit what you have asked, but think it over well, and you will find that truth may be hidden too deeply for it to be seen at the first glance.

What Cupid Tells

Upright

1. This love is true.

2. Not yet. There will be some delay.

3. Your own heart should answer.

4. Yes, but make sure of your own mind.

5. All is well.

6. If you lose at love, it will be your own fault.

7. A loved one is unhappy because of you.

8. Beware of jealousy; it is a shadow between you two.

9. You alone are loved.

10. A love interest is thinking of you now.

11. The cloud will pass.

12. Someone has changed his or her mind.

13. Yes, but it will not be the one you mean.

14. Why should you doubt?

15. Remember his or her words as you parted.

16. The love is true.

Reversed

1. The person does not agree with you in many things. Think well.

2. Not the sort to be deceived easily.

3. Do not listen to those who flatter you. That way danger lies.

4. You would forgive if you knew the truth.

5. Your judgment has been harsh.

6. If love is true, it will face misfortune.

7. Do not judge from appearances.

8. A friend who loves you truly.

9. Too fond of amusements.

10. A flirt. Beware.

11. There is a misunderstanding on both sides.

12. Nasty tongues, nasty minds.

13. Do not act in haste.

14. Forget that infatuation.

15. There is no cause for jealousy.

16. Be wise in time.

26

The Spell of the New Moon

Ask whatever question you choose, so long as it concerns your relatives, your friends, or your home.

Shut your eyes and turn this book three times, keeping it open at this page. Keep your mind fixed on the question you are going to ask. Then, with your eyes still shut, try to touch one of the figures in the tablet with your finger or a pencil or other pointer. If the pointer falls outside the tablet, there is no reply today. Try again tomorrow. But should the pointer touch one of the figures, turn to the answers, and against the corresponding number you will find your reply.

At first sight, the reply may not seem to fit what you have asked, but think it over well, and you will find that truth may be hidden too deeply for it to be seen at the first glance.

What the New Moon Says

Upright

1. Be patient. All is well.
2. There is trouble, but the fault is yours.
3. Do not worry about him or her.
4. Love will find a way.
5. It is a matter of jealousy.
6. You are fanciful.
7. A fair woman.
8. It is very unlikely.
9. A disappointment concerns what is in your mind.
10. Hot words cause regret.
11. The suspicions are unfounded.
12. A splendid friend is there to help.
13. You ought to be content.
14. A near neighbor is your true friend.
15. Your wish will be granted.
16. A removal.

Reversed

1. The worst enemy is yourself.
2. Less than ever.
3. If you can, do so with a clear conscience.
4. There will be none.
5. It is possible that it will come to pass.
6. None, if you use discretion.
7. Sometimes, but very seldom.
8. Something will happen to alter things for the better.
9. You will do more harm than good.
10. Do not confide in any of them.
11. They are talking against you.
12. Your secret is not safe.
13. One who speaks her mind is to be trusted.
14. It will not last long.
15. You have no cause to doubt.
16. All is for the best.

27

The Spell of the Rising Sun

Ask any question you choose, so long as it concerns time.

Shut your eyes and turn this book three times, keeping it open at this page. Keep your mind fixed on the question you are going to ask. Then, with your eyes still shut, try to touch one of the figures in the tablet with your finger or a pencil or other pointer. If the pointer falls outside the tablet, there is no reply today. Try again tomorrow. But should the pointer touch one of the figures, turn to the answers, and against the corresponding number you will find your reply.

At first sight, the reply may not seem to fit what you have asked, but think it over well, and you will find that truth may be hidden too deeply for it to be seen at the first glance

The Rising Sun Gives Your Answer

Upright

1. In six months.
2. Never.
3. It will come to pass shortly.
4. Not just yet.
5. Go forward and prosper.
6. Sooner than you expect.
7. Before the year has ended.
8. Yes.
9. Something causes delay.
10. Impatience is your fault.
11. At once.
12. Very soon indeed.
13. Look for your lucky day.
14. You have not long to wait.
15. There seems no chance of it coming to pass.
16. A year from now.

Reversed

1. Wait seven days.
2. In a fortnight.
3. Time will tell.
4. Not for a long time.
5. Wait.
6. The change will be very slow.
7. The hundredth day of the year.
8. The fifteenth of the month.
9. Not for two years.
10. Never.
11. Days may run into months.
12. Three times.
13. Much sooner than you think.
14. Leave things as they are as long as possible.
15. Very unlikely.
16. Quite soon.

28 The Lucky Bell

Ask any question you choose, so long as it concerns a letter or e-mail correspondence, whether it is one you have sent or one you are expecting.

Shut your eyes and turn this book three times, keeping it open at this page. Keep your mind fixed on the question you are going to ask. Then, with eyes still shut, try to touch one of the figures in the tablet with your finger or a pencil or other pointer. If the pointer falls outside the tablet, there is no reply today. Try again tomorrow. But should the pointer touch one of the figures, turn to the answers, and against the corresponding number you will find your reply.

At first sight, the reply may not seem to fit what you have asked, but think it over well, and you will find that truth may be hidden too deeply for it to be seen at the first glance.

Listen to the Voice of the Bell

Upright

1. Yes, but there will be delay.
2. It will be here soon.
3. It is doubtful that you will hear, but the thoughts of someone are on you.
4. You will have a response but not the one you expect.
5. A disappointment.
6. Good news.
7. Not yet. Have patience a little while.
8. The silence will be explained.
9. Do not worry. It is not worthwhile.
10. Money is coming.
11. It is a pity you did not write before.
12. Your wish is to be granted.
13. The silence is ending.
14. It tells of true love.
15. Not for a little while.
16. You are impatient.

Reversed

1. Write at once.
2. Not for some time.
3. Write what is in your heart. It is no time for false pride.
4. The words did not mean what you thought.
5. There will be none.
6. There is good reason for the delay.
7. Write by all means, but do so cautiously.
8. The one you expect will be followed by others.
9. A full explanation is forthcoming.
10. Absolutely.
11. Much nearer than you think.
12. From far away.
13. Beyond doubt.
14. Yes, and you will be glad about it.
15. It will show that you have made a mistake.
16. At once.

143

The Magnetic Horseshoe

29

Ask any question you like that is connected with a journey that either you or a friend may think of taking.

Shut your eyes and turn this book three times, keeping it open at this page. Keep your mind fixed on the question you are going to ask. Then, with your eyes still shut, try to touch one of the figures in the tablet with your finger or a pencil or other pointer. If the pointer falls outside the tablet, there is no reply today. Try again tomorrow. But should the pointer touch one of the figures, turn to the answers, and against the corresponding number you will find your reply.

At first sight, the reply may not seem to fit what you have asked, but think it over well, and you will find that truth may be hidden too deeply for it to be seen at the first glance.

The Horseshoe Draws Thoughts from Afar

Upright

1. Not yet.
2. Yes, it is for the best.
3. You had better remain where you are.
4. A long journey is ahead.
5. Thoughts from afar are on you.
6. A disappointment.
7. Only a short distance.
8. Yes, but it is not important.
9. The world is small in these days of fast travel.
10. It will be very sudden.
11. Certainly for the better.
12. Many changes are at hand.
13. What you hope for will happen.
14. Wait a little longer.
15. All for the best.
16. Do not go.

Reversed

1. Wishes to be with you.
2. It is not to be advised.
3. You will refuse.
4. When you least expect it.
5. Some gain, some loss.
6. It should be soon.
7. A very pleasant time.
8. Think carefully first.
9. It is more than doubtful.
10. It will lead to happiness, but not in the way you think.
11. Toward the West.
12. It will not be all happiness.
13. The distance is great.
14. Before very long.
15. The East is calling.
16. Not yet.

33 Ways to Tell Your Future

The Scales of Fate

30

Ask any question you choose, so long as it is concerned with some wrong that ought to be righted or with some doubt in your mind you long to have set at rest.

Shut your eyes and turn this book three times, keeping it open at this page. Keep your mind fixed on the question you are going to ask. Then, with your eyes still shut, try to touch one of the figures in the tablet with your finger or a pencil or other pointer. If the pointer falls outside the tablet, there is no reply today. Try again tomorrow. But should the pointer touch one of the figures, turn to the answers, and against the corresponding number you will find your reply.

At first sight, the reply may not seem to fit what you have asked, but think it over well, and you will find that truth may be hidden too deeply for it to be seen at the first glance.

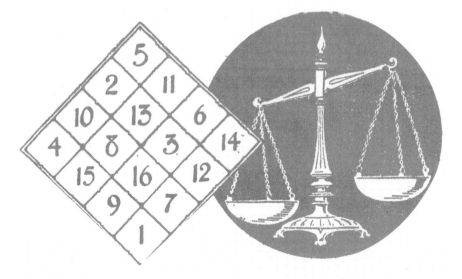

Here Justice Speaks

Upright

1. You have been misjudged or you are misjudging.
2. The truth will come to light.
3. Your judgment was too hasty.
4. The cloud will pass.
5. You are quite wrong.
6. Most certainly you are right.
7. Your own experience should teach you.
8. You know the truth already. Why ask?
9. No one can reply to your question.
10. You will not have long to wait.
11. Try again.
12. You need not fear.
13. Yes, but right will triumph.
14. Things are not so bad as you fear.
15. It is an affair of foolish scandal.
16. You have been wrong.

Reversed

1. Your judgment was hasty.
2. You will not be one of the principals.
3. It looks as if you could not escape the trouble.
4. An improvement quite soon.
5. Be brave; you have done no harm.
6. A cruel injustice.
7. Be more cautious.
8. There is no danger.
9. Justice must triumph in the end.
10. You are foolish to be afraid.
11. Speak without fear.
12. No, which is a good thing.
13. You are not mistaken.
14. Make all plans slowly and with due thought.
15. There is no need for anxiety.
16. All will come right.

31 The Seal of Solomon

Ask any question you choose, so long as it concerns a big building or someone who is connected to such a place. The building may be a court, office building, mall, cinema, theater, hospital, church, or public building of any sort.

Shut your eyes and turn this book three times, keeping it open at this page. Keep your mind fixed on the question you are going to ask. Then, with your eyes still shut, try to touch one of the figures in the tablet with your finger or a pencil or other pointer. If the pointer falls outside the tablet, there is no reply today. Try again tomorrow. But should the pointer touch one of the figures, turn to the answers, and against the corresponding number you will find your reply.

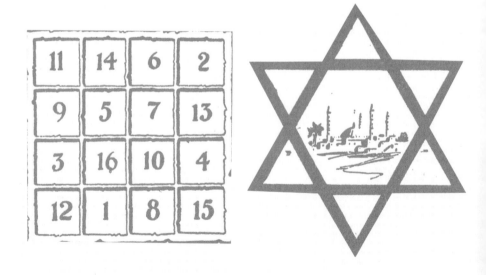

11	14	6	2
9	5	7	13
3	16	10	4
12	1	8	15

Here Your Question Is Answered

Upright

1. A friend is waiting for you there.

2. Happiness.

3. New work or new hope is there.

4. Gaiety.

5. Someone within the walls thinks of you.

6. Disappointment.

7. Be brave. All is for the best.

8. Yes, but not the place you think.

9. Under watchful eyes.

10. Seek another large building. A little thought will tell you where.

11. A surprise awaits you there.

12. All is well.

13. Good news waits for you.

14. You pass it every day.

15. Every hope will be fulfilled.

16. A strange place.

Reversed

1. Avoid the place. You know it well.

2. It was never a secret. Many people know.

3. There is more sadness than pleasure waiting.

4. Not to be trusted.

5. What you expect will happen.

6. Yes, but the fault will not be yours.

7. Jealousy makes a dark cloud.

8. Unjust suspicions are afloat.

9. One of a number of friends.

10. Machinery or electronics is concerned with the place. One who tends it is thinking of you.

11. Enjoy yourself and don't worry.

12. A rather unpleasant experience is at hand.

13. Only a trifle that will be forgotten.

14. Don't be frivolous.

15. Be careful what you say.

16. Turn the other way.

The Seal of Solomon

32 The Tablet of the Sphinx

Ask any question. What will the tablet tell me today?

Shut your eyes and turn this book three times, keeping it open at this page. Keep your mind fixed on the question you are going to ask. Then, with your eyes still shut, try to touch one of the figures in the tablet with your finger or a pencil or other pointer. If the pointer falls outside the tablet there is no reply today. Try again tomorrow. But should the pointer touch one of the figures, turn to the answers, and against the corresponding number you will find your reply.

Should the reply be favorable, turn to the other tablets that deal with what you have in your mind. Otherwise, wait until the Sphinx assures you that the time is right. The tablets should not be consulted more than once a day, nor should the same question be asked by the same person more than once a week.

You have consulted the Sphinx and discovered that today is a fortunate one for your questionings. At first sight, the reply may not seem to fit what you have asked, but think it over well, and you will find that truth may be hidden too deeply for it to be seen at the first glance.

The Sphinx Replies

Upright

1. Put your fate to the test right now.
2. Tomorrow will be better.
3. Thursday is the day.
4. You are too impatient. Wait.
5. Sunday.
6. Do not delay.
7. The answers are ready.
8. Tuesday.
9. On what day were you born? Try on that day.
10. Saturday would be better.
11. There is nothing to be told.
12. Monday will be fortunate.
13. Do not hesitate.
14. Try on Friday.
15. Wednesday.
16. At once.

Reversed

1. It is not advisable today.
2. Yes, at once.
3. Any day but Thursday.
4. Leave it as it is.
5. No, not on Sunday.
6. Wait seven days.
7. Do not try at all.
8. Wait until next week.
9. Before very long if you keep your temper.
10. Not on any Saturday.
11. Secrets wait.
12. Monday is unfortunate in this connection.
13. Make sure of your own mind before you try.
14. Good fortune waits.
15. Certainly not.
16. Not at all.

The Tablet of the Sphinx

33 The Symbolic Coin

Ask any question you like, so long as it is concerning business, work, or money.

Shut your eyes and turn this book three times, keeping it open at this page. Keep your mind fixed on the questions you are going to ask. Then, with your eyes still closed, try to touch one of the figures on the tablet with your finger or a pencil or other pointer. If the pointer falls outside the tablet, there is no reply today. Try again tomorrow. But should the pointer touch one of the figures, turn to the answers, and against the corresponding number you will find your reply.

At first sight, the reply may not seem to fit what you have asked, but think it over well, and you will find that truth may be hidden too deeply for it to be seen at first glance.

The coin is the symbol of success; here are its replies to your question.

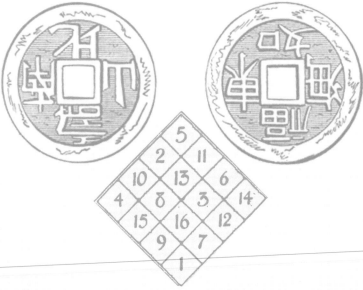

The Symbolic Coin Replies

Upright

1. Many changes.
2. Fresh work.
3. It rests with you.
4. Better happiness than wealth.
5. The dark time is nearly over.
6. A great surprise.
7. You had better think well before you agree.
8. Hard work is required.
9. Show how you are to be trusted.
10. Take great care.
11. There are difficulties ahead.
12. You anxiety will soon be ended.
13. Good luck is coming.
14. Don't be fainthearted.
15. All is well.
16. Be patient.

Reversed

1. Loss of money is better than loss of friends.
2. It will cost a great deal.
3. The risk is considerable.
4. Do not count on it.
5. Riches are waiting.
6. Be prepared to face some blame.
7. You are looking at it from the wrong point of view.
8. Beware of selfishness. There are others in the world.
9. No one can prevent the success if you persevere.
10. Turn back.
11. Second thoughts are best.
12. Just what you deserve.
13. Money.
14. The change will be for the better.
15. An accident will be to your advantage.
16. Do not be afraid.

About the Authors

Internationally known self-help author Monte Farber's inspiring guidance and empathic insights impact everyone he encounters. Amy Zerner's exquisite, one-of-a-kind spiritual couture creations and collaged fabric paintings exude her profound intuition and deep connection with archetypal stories, color, and healing energies. She sells her one-of-a-kind creations exclusively through Bergdorf Goodman in New York City.

For more than thirty years, Amy and Monte have combined their deep love for each other with the work of inner exploration and self-discovery to build The Enchanted World of Amy Zerner and Monte Farber: books, card decks, and oracles that have helped millions answer questions, find deeper meaning, and follow their own spiritual paths.

Together they've made their love for each other a work of art and their art the work of their lives. Their best-selling titles include *The Chakra Meditation Kit*, *The Tarot Discovery Kit*, *Karma Cards*, *The Enchanted Spellboard*, *Secrets of the Fortune Bell*, *Little Reminders: Love & Relationships*, *Little Reminders: The Law of Attraction*, *Goddess, Guide Me!*, *The Animal Powers Meditation Kit*, *Astrology Gems*, *True Love Tarot*, *The Enchanted Tarot*, *The Instant Tarot Reader*, *The Psychic Circle*, *The Pathfinder Psychic Talking Board*, *The Truth Fairy*, *The Ghostwriter Automatic Writing Kit*, *Spirit of the Ancestors Altar Kit*, *The Mystic Messenger*, *Wish Upon a Star*, *The Breathe Easy Deck*, *The Healing Deck*, *Healing Crystals*, *The Zerner/Farber Tarot Deck*, and *Tarot Secrets*.

Visit their Web site: www.TheEnchantedWorld.com

LUCK

"The best way to predict your future is to create it!"

—Abraham Lincoln